HOW TO LIVE & WORK

In this Series

How to Choose a Private School
How to Claim State Benefits
How to Enjoy Retirement
How to Get a Job Abroad
How to Get That Job
How to Help Your Child at School
How to Keep Business Accounts
How to Live & Work in America
How to Live & Work in Australia
How to Pass Exams Without Anxiety
How to Raise Business Finance
How to Run a Club or Society
How to Survive at College
How to Use a Library
How to Write That Book

other titles in preparation

LIVE & WORK
IN AUSTRALIA

Laura Veltman

Northcote House

Acknowledgements

I would like to acknowledge the help in this project of many friends and 'all the family'. Special thanks to Sonya Veltman, Duncan Pinkerton, Penny Griffith, Amanda Paxton, as well as Murray Hedgcock and Tony Boyd. Thanks also to officers of the Australian High Commission in London and Australia's State and Territory governments for assistance with information.

© Laura Veltman 1987.

First published in 1987 by Northcote House Publishers Ltd, Harper & Row House, Estover Road, Plymouth PL6 7PZ, United Kingdom. Tel: Plymouth (0752) 705251. Telex: 45635. Fax: (0752) 777603.

Reprinted 1988 and 1989.

British Library Cataloguing in Publication Data
Veltman, Laura
    How to live and work in Australia. ____
    (How to books).
    1. Australia ____ Handbooks, manuals, etc.
    I. Title
    919.4'0463   DU95

    ISBN 0-7463-0331-9

Typeset by St. George Typesetting, Commercial Centre,
Wilson Way, Pool Industrial Estate, Redruth, Cornwall. TR15 3QT.
Printed and bound in Great Britain.

Contents

1
First: The Good News

There are so many tall tales about Australia — including the myth that it's 'impossible' to get in. Yet doors are positively flung open to the 'right' kind of people, with an awareness of how to present their case. For Australia unblushingly seeks to skim off the cream of applicants from other countries. Despite changes of governments and minor hiccups in its migration policy, the number of people allowed in has increased in recent years, and now stands at over 100,000 annually. No more is it necessary to have a very close relative or a job waiting for you Down Under.

- Perhaps you are thinking of leaving the uncertainties and rigidities of your home behind, and restarting a career or business in a better place?
- Maybe the notion of almost year-long warmth and sunshine appeals to your body and spirit? Do you hope to live and work in an environment like Australia's on a temporary basis — either for the adventure or as a test run?
- Do you have family living there who you'd like to join when you retire, or are you considering the move to Australia as a chance to change your lifestyle, while investing your financial assets so you can afford to live well, without having a regular job?
- Is there a course of study you'd like to take in one of the many universities or tertiary colleges Down Under? Are you planning to travel the country in your holidays? Or do you have friends and relatives you'd like to see, while earning money on an extended working holiday?

The world sees Australia in an evermore positive light, as a desirable place to live in or just to visit. For their part, Australians are more open to newcomers than the stereotype image may have led you to believe.

These days migrants are widely recognised as a boon both socially and economically.

However, the red tape and high application fees can be daunting for would-be temporary or permanent settlers — and neither your time nor your money will be refunded if you are rejected.

It is vital to be well prepared for the form-filling and interviews demanded by the application procedure, as well as to know what to expect at the other side. This book aims to be an entertaining guide to gaining residency and work permits. It also seeks to dispel some post-arrival fairy tales — and portray the living, social, education and business conditions you and your family might reasonably expect on making a move to Australia. So, before Australia makes up its mind about you, consider carefully whether *your* expectations of the place, people and lifestyle are realistic.

Fairy tales from the Land of Oz

Question: How can you tell that a planeload of moygrants is on the landing strip at Sinney Airport? *Answer:* After the engines switch off, the whining goes on...

After 200 years' experience of newcomers, Australians have a veritable library of jokes about 'whining' immigrants. New arrivals have some dreams which come true and others which are swept away when they are confronted with real life Down Under.

Homesickness or culture shock are common reasons for complaints and rejection of life in Australia. After coping successfully with the hassles of migrating, a small number of people find themselves so traumatised they feel obliged to leave. Inability to make 'a go of it' in Australia — or in any unfamiliar environment — is often due to insufficient planning of the move in advance.

The prevailing long-distance view of one of the Western World's most sought-after destinations is one of Ockers and Sheilas, Paul Hogans and Dame Ednas. So people who seriously consider living in Australia are often misled by myths. If you have never lived there, or simply visited as a tourist, Australia could seem a land of sunny opportunities which — like the endless backyard swimming pools you see as your plane comes in to land at any Australian city — go on and on.   Can you smell prawns sizzling on the barbecue, taste the cold beer and feel that fat (and regularly-indexed) pay-packet in your pocket? Many dream of a country where lucky citizens occasionally take a break from sunshine, beaches and outdoor sporting events with sprees in luxurious (air-conditioned) shopping centres, tucking into lobster at a seafront restaurant, or to spend time in the local pub, club, disco or theatre. Of course the work ethic is a quirk of the 'old country', a weird nightmare, according to the popular mythology about the Land of Oz.

Those ready to wrestle with the Aussie 'slanguage', adopt the local drawl, embrace the notion of a classless society, and revel in the Great Outdoors (humidity, flies, mosquitoes notwithstanding), may conclude Australia is paradise... remote from the threat of war, a permanent holiday on earth,and a land for adventurers convinced their 'old world' is running out of steam.

Such is the legend of life Down Under.

However, if seriously thinking about moving to a place you naturally hope is a better place to live, put the myths aside (no need to forget them entirely — since there's more than a grain of truth in most Aussie fairy-tales) and consider the *facts* of Australian life...warts 'n' all.

Australia's 'New Immigrant'

Many international personalities — like England cricket star Ian Botham, and Irish popstar and famine fund-raiser Bob Geldof — have proclaimed Australia as an ideal place to live. They, like a host of other celebrities, have given credence to the image of Australia as a place that's particularly pleasant and healthy for themselves and their families if they ever decided to emigrate. Many of the mega-rich from the United States, Europe and Britain visit regularly or have holiday homes Down Under.

Yet it's worth noting about 20,000 people *leave* Australia each year, to return to countries they have emigrated from or because they are Aussies who would rather live and work elsewhere. Consider how many famous Australians have moved away and find the thought of actually having to live in their birthplace unpalatable, even traumatic. Why have people like media magnate Rupert Murdoch, comedienne Pamela Stephenson, feminist writer Germaine Greer, entertainer Barry Humphries, and media star Clive James spent years of their lives elsewhere — or even given up their citizenship rights entirely?

In some ways, the wife of cricket star Ian Botham summed up the drawbacks of living in this place which so many former residents see as a nice place to visit, but a bit dull in the long term. Late in 1986, when Botham was keen to take up a lucrative cricketing contract to live and work (temporarily) in Queensland, his wife Kathy said from back home in Yorkshire, England: "I spent four months in Australia once, and I was sick of all that blue sky and sunshine. I couldn't wait to get home." Which proves that you can't please all the New Australians all the time.

Immigration targets

Historically the migration philosophy was motivated by a 'populate or

perish' paranoia. Until the 1950s, the idea was to gain quantity rather
than quality through mass arrivals of what polite Australian society still
calls New Australians (and what the irreverent and downright rude call
wops, wogs and poms).

Australia's land mass accounts for a quarter of the entire Asian-
Pacific region, but it contains only about half of one per cent of the
population. As in the beginning of mass migration to Australia, many
settlers came from Britain though these days newcomers from the Asian
region are increasing. There are also large numbers of people of Middle
Eastern, Southern European, Central and South American and African
origins, including refugees, adding to the cultural mix. About half of
Australia's immigrant population is British by birth, and the next biggest
ethnic groups established there are Italian, Greek and Yugoslav.

About four million immigrants from 120 countries have made their
homes there since World War Two, mostly in the decade or so after it.
Intake reduced sharply in the early 1950s due to a sudden paranoia
associated with the Cold War and Australia's isolated position as a
largely white, Christian outpost in the Asian-Pacific region.

Supporters of what became known as the White Australia policy
displayed all the grudges of other isolated and, therefore, xenophobic
societies — like racism.

More reasonable opponents of wholesale migration — many trade
unionists among them — argued the influx of 'cheap' workers would
undermine their jobs by accepting low wages and living conditions
repellent to 'dinky-di' Aussies. Too many people would lower the quality
of life, deplete the stock of natural resources and retard economic
growth. They'd be housed and then kept by the welfare state, said the
anti-migration lobby of the old school.

There was strong support for this overtly racist White Australian
policy. It was and sometimes still is supported by many Australians —
including those who, ironically, were themselves once refugees or poor
workers from Britain and Europe as well as by 'dinky-dis' afraid of the
country being overrun by the 'yellow peril' from over-populated Asian
countries to the north.

However, the current policy of encouraging the 'right' kind of migrant
is based on a fresh profile of the Ideal Migrant. No longer are they
encouraged to 'blend in' as part of a uniform social wallpaper. Nor is
there a government tendency to ignore ethnic interest groups in the hope
they'll assimilate, as does the United States with its melting-pot
philosophy of ethnicity.

In Australia, the buzzword is 'multiculturalism'. Australia's new
citizens are given financial and social incentives to retain the lifestyles,
languages and the artistic traditions of 'the old country.' Since the White

Australia policy was scrapped in the early 1970s by a new Labor Party national government under Prime Minister Gough Whitlam, the ideal of allowing immigrants to nourish a newish nation with the best of their respective cultures appears to be a success.

In New South Wales the latest appointee to the sensitive job of adviser to the State Premier on ethnic affairs is former Vietnamese refugee Mr Hop Van Chu. He explained multiculturalism this way: "If you deny a person's ethnic background by expecting him or her to blend in, you deny individuality. Minorities feel excluded from society and ashamed of their backgrounds. How can such a society expect their loyalty? As a result of multiculturalism, Australians are increasingly comfortable with the diversity of fellow-citizens."

In the mid-1980s a restructuring of the immigration policy and expansion of migrant quotas reflected a more positive attitude to the value of newcomers bringing the best of their old worlds with them. The election of a Labor Government under Prime Minister Bob Hawke meant an effort to kill two birds with one stone:

- show the Government to be remedying the population shortage by selecting people with skills and money to come to Australia, who
- are therefore *un*likely to be a burden on the welfare system.

Chris Hurford, the Minister for Immigration in the Hawke Government until 1987, summed up the rules as they now apply: "We need some migrants as much as many of them need Australia. Any sound investment, be it in capital or human terms, provides the best returns over many years. Immigration is an investment in human capital."

"...I was sick of all that blue sky and sunshine..."

2
Great Expectations

Studies show there are basic differences in the type of people inclined to migrate — and those who would never consider such a drastic step. The theory is that the tendency to migrate, if you have it, springs from psychological type. Your original environment may stimulate this desire, but would not be enough to push you away from familiar ground if you weren't that type in the first place. People prone to migrate are, according to a report by the Australian Department of Immigration and Ethnic Affairs in 1983:

"...counter-phobic, preoccupied with ego skills, have only loose social relationships and are competitive and self-reliant. They display only superficial ties wth surrounding people and objects. Those who are not emigration-prone are characterised by exaggerated ties with familiar things and cling to them at all costs."

Immigration experts talk of 'pull and push factors' when they discuss reasons why people like you may be attracted to the idea of changing your life by going to Australia for more than just a holiday or family get-together. A typical push factor for some people is the idea of yet another gloomy European winter — or even one more cold, wet summer. Another important push factor for the migration-prone is lack of economic opportunity due to so many people competing for a small piece of the available action. High costs in housing, food, heating, and relatively low wages are strong push factors from the more depressed regions of Britain or Europe.

For would-be immigrants to Australia from warm but overcrowded nations in South-East Asia or Southern Europe, the lure of wide-open spaces Down Under is a motivating force.

'Pull' factors are all the optimistic notions of daily life in ideal countries like Australia, Canada or the United States. The-grass-is-greener-on-the-other-side syndrome is particularly prevalent in the case of Australia. The whole world has heard of the violence of American cities through news and the movies, and is aware that frozen winters are a feature of life in Canada but not in Australia, where most of the nation's 16 million people live in warm seaside suburbs.

Non-nuclear
Another important reason for choosing Australia is fear of nuclear pollution or — more terrifying still — of nuclear war, obliterating their homes and poisoning the environment in the Northern Hemisphere especially. Recent accidents at nuclear plants in Europe and the United States have contributed to the attraction of Australia, which has no nuclear stations now and none planned. However, Australia does have the world's largest deposits of uranium. Export of this raw material to stoke nuclear plants and projects elsewhere is a burning political question.

Family Reunion
Another major 'pull' factor is the desire to join friends and relatives who have moved Down Under already. A family to advise you, to help with the application for temporary or permanent residence, and to ease the transition to a totally different environment and culture should be a wonderful advantage in terms of your application.

Since nearly half the people in Australia came as immigrants or are themselves the children of immigrants, the government's policy remains heavily biased toward 'family reunion' on humanitarian grounds. Family Reunion is a specific category for people with close relatives in Australia. It accounts for over a quarter of the people who migrate there each year.

Tolerance of immigrants
Franca Arena, a politician and a leader of Australia's ethnic community, speaks from her own experience about what newcomers can expect in Australia. She arrived in 1959 from Genoa in Italy: "Moving from one country to another is a great trauma — even if you are not a refugee and have a job to go to, relatives to help you, a place to stay and are able to speak the language," she says. "Australia today is a tolerant, sophisticated society with some of the best back-up facilities for immigrants and minority groups in the world. There is an ethnic affairs commission and equal opportunity employment office set up by the governments of most States. Interpreters, English classes for adults and children, assessment of overseas qualifications and general advice services are other features of Australia's services for migrants."

The fact that Mr Hop Van Chu, a chemical engineer and MBA (Master of Business Administration, Drexel University, Philadelphia, USA) has his present job at all shows the power of the immigrant voice in Australia. As the adviser to the New South Wales Premier on the impact of government policies on ethnic groups, he represents the influence of minority groups. Politicians across the country regularly refer to the 'migrant vote' — crucial in some areas.

Culture shock

Mr Hop declares the 'shock' to newcomers to Australia is cushioned for those already familiar with the British or Western lifestyle. "For Oriental people (who represent a significant proportion of new immigrants) the attitudes of children to parents is a major difference." He agrees with Franca Arena that Indo-Chinese immigrants — including former Vietnamese refugees like himself — bear the brunt of discrimination against ethnic minorities. He admits this is not pleasant: "People in metropolitan areas like Sydney or Melbourne accept the presence of Oriental and other ethnic minorities as just another facet of life. But people in rural areas more often find it a discomfort and say there are too many Asians here."

Another prominent New Australian, Dr Alessandra Pucci, who heads one of the world's leading biotechnology companies specialising in pharmaceutical and agricultural applications, adds: "It is a major shock when you are starting out in a new place and so totally ignorant of the culture. At first, it may be difficult to appreciate how much Australia can have to offer."

3
Australia — The Making of a Nation

Convict transportation

Australia's modern history began with an influx of people who didn't want to be there. The first Europeans who came to live and work in Australia were convicts and their guardians. Australia, so alluring nowadays for tourists and emigrants, was a place for the disposal of the criminal elements of Georgian and Victorian England and old fashioned histories politely refer to its first decades as 'colourful.' More modern, X-rated versions have facts aplenty to show that, from 1787 to 1868, the colony was little more than Britain's social sewer. According to the experts, between half and two-thirds of the convict transportees were violent criminals while four out of five were thieves. According to historian Robert Hughes: "People used to supress convict history in the 19th century because it was thought to be a disgusting stain and an inherent disgrace on the Australian genes."

Today, some Australians will tell you they descend from convicts and are proud of it, because their ancestors were free-thinkers sent from Mother England as political prisoners. In truth, the first transports of people deemed undesirable for political reasons did not arrive in Australia until well into the 19th century.

New frontiers

Eventually the lower and middle classes back in England got wind that this colony was not necessarily a hell hole. Newspaper and personal reports soon spread the word that adventurers as well as convicts who had finished their sentences were doing very nicely, thank you, on their own bits of bush or in fledgling townships. Though distant as the moon, and despite its rough social fabric, the colony gained a reputation as a fine place to make a fresh start or even a fortune. In 1851 gold was discovered in Victoria, leading to a blast of prosperity parallel to the gold rush of North America. Plenty of arable land plus a vested interest in the quality of their new society resulted in 'anti-transportation' leagues persuading Britain to dump its criminals elsewhere. The last convict transport ship arrived in 1868, at Fremantle in Western Australia.

Much folklore and history arises from the push to explore the interior of this vast continent. The pioneering attitude of thousands of free civilians from Britain and Europe is still evident among people living and moving there today.

A cynical legacy

However, 20th century Australia still has some of the characteristics of the island jail. People tend to be on the cynical side about those who run their country. Many take it for granted that politics and organised crime may go hand in hand. Politicians, police and other figures of authority like judges often have trouble commanding respect and are generally low on the scale of professions, in terms of public prestige. Regular revelations about unions, 'pollies' (politicians), police and the law being on the take, or otherwise crooked, reinforce an impression at home and abroad that 'Godzone' country is politically, judicially or morally nothing like perfect.

A walk through the sleazier streets of Sydney, Melbourne or outback mining communities demonstrates vice is alive and kicking...while police cars cruise by. Yet, while cynics suspect that crooked activities emerging publicly are the tip of an iceberg, others say this proves the sound health of Australia's democracy, because such big scandals come to light at all.

Australia's political system

In Australia democracy means hopping into the front seat beside your taxi driver or chauffeur. Egalitarianism translates as ''aving a go' behind the steering wheel as well — providing your driver can be trusted not to complain to the union and start a demarcation dispute.

At first glance, Australia's politics and law may appear a complicated bastard, bewigged and gowned in vestiges of Britain's Westminster system. A closer inspection reveals the nation has adapted some of the best features of systems for law, order and democracy evolved by British, North American and Western European societies. In these other places the wheels of justice and politics may clank'n'grind medieval-style, shackling the present to past centuries of recorded history. Australia, on the other hand, has a mere 200 years of Western civilisation to draw on, no traditional ruling class, and certain advantages in geographic isolation. So it can afford to be selective about the bits of government it adopts, while free to fit other features to the circumstances. The influence of political convicts from Britain made it one of the first countries in the world with universal suffrage and Australia remains a most progressive democracy.

Politically, Australia's history began with colonies on the eastern coast at Sydney harbour, a few miles inland at Parramatta, then north to Brisbane and south to Melbourne, Tasmania and Adelaide. Gradually the colony expanded westward and divided into various States which achieved federation on the first day of the 20th century — 1st January 1901. There is a Prime Minister at Federal (national) level, and Premiers heading the cabinet of each State parliament, except for the Northern Territory which has a Chief Minister.

The monarch of Great Britain and Ireland is also King or Queen of Australia. The British monarch's representative at national level is the Governor-General, and each State has its own Governor, with ceremonial duties as the monarch's representative.

Constitutional crisis in 1975

In 1975 the then Governor-General Sir John Kerr exerted the monarch's paper power to dissolve the Federal parliament against the wishes of the Labor Prime Minister Gough Whitlam. This plunged a politically easygoing nation into a constitutional crisis and strained relations with the British monarchy.

Agitation for severance of the last links with British royalty has gained momentum ever since. A strong argument in favour of republicanism is based on the fact that so many Australians have no personal or even cultural ties to Britain, due to the vast influx of immigrants from elsewhere after World War Two. So far, the republican push has been gratified on a legal level only: appeals to the Privy Council in London ended after 1983, when the Labor government of Prime Minister Bob Hawke won office. Now Australia's High Court has the final word within the nation's judicial system.

Three tiers of government

The Federal (or Commonwealth) Government is based in Canberra, a city designed, like Washington DC, as an administrative centre for the federation of States and Territories. The parliament in Canberra has a House of Representatives and a States' house — known as the Senate — to which a certain number of senators are elected from each State and the Northern Territory. Citizens and enfranchised residents (over the age of 18) are obliged to cast their votes at elections held every three years.

Territory and State governments are the second tier of government. This is where the Australian system of democracy becomes complicated. Apart from confusion for a newcomer used to one parliament for a democratic country, Australians must cope with eight. Because the Federal Government has the job of making decisions on matters affecting the whole country, its elected representatives crop up continually in State affairs. Meanwhile, politicians in the States wrangle with Canberra. Many aim to boost their careers with a transfer to seats in the Federal Parliament. Australia's federal system therefore makes party tactics and internal politics especially volatile for those at the hub. And no wonder so many other citizens don't bother to keep up with changing faces and policies running the nation.

In the late 1980s, the States of New South Wales, Victoria, South Australia, Western Australia as well as the Federal Parliament are run by Australian Labor Party governments. Queensland, the Northern Territory and Tasmania have Liberal or National Party conservatives at the helm.

The Australian constitution gives the Federal Parliament — via its administrative wing, the Commonwealth public service — responsibility for defence, migration, social services, overseas and interstate trade and national economic law. It also gives it powers to legislate on banking, currency, raising of loans abroad, income and other taxation. Much of the taxation revenue is siphoned back to the States so the politicians in Canberra have influence over education, health care, road building, and funding for the arts at State level.

If Commonwealth and State laws clash, Commonwealth legislation must take precedence. State governments, each with their own public service, have the constitutional right to make laws on matters not covered by the Commonwealth authorities in Canberra. The States are generally responsible for education, transport links, forests and conservation, water and mineral resources, hospitals, community services, urban and industrial infrastructure. Though the Federal Government has a fair grip on the purse strings for such services through its income-tax raising powers, the States finance their activities through other kinds of taxes and loans raised outside the country. Stamp duty and charges on financial transactions and banking are key devices used by State governments to keep themselves in business. The taxation system is discussed in detail in Chapter 9.

The State governments of New South Wales, Victoria, South Australia, Western Australia and Tasmania each have their own constitutions and a parliament of two houses, a legislative assembly (the lower house) and a legislative council (the upper house) — Queensland has only the lower house, or legislative assembly. The Australian Capital Territory (including Canberra) has an Advisory Council while the Northern Territory has a legislative assembly.

By making policies on land, agriculture and environment within their borders, the States find themselves overseeing the establishment of new industry and business, thus wielding some power over questions of immigration. State and territory governments advise Canberra of shortages in particular skills or professions, and the viability of proposed investments or businesses by foreigners or would-be immigrants.

Local government
There is a third tier of government. Shire, municipal or city councils run Australia's urban and rural regions. These are responsible for town planning, sewerage, garbage collection, maintaining roads and bridges as well as community facilities like public libraries. Local governments finance their activities through land and water rates or similar charges on households and businesses in their areas. Financially, local councils are partly dependent on funding from the States.

Economy: still the lucky country?
Australians had a shock when their acid-tongued Federal Treasurer, Paul Keating, tried to pull the beach towel from under them. In 1986 he told them Australia was no longer 'the lucky country' and its easygoing society was heading for the economic rocks. Australia would wind up a banana republic, he warned, unless the locals changed their attitudes to work, wages and consumption.

Treasurer Keating's words have set the tone for Australia into the 1990s, though most Australians tend to take the typically 'she'll be right' attitude and ignore the creeping costs which economic problems have imposed on individual lifestyles.

However, those who travel abroad, who depend on import/export business for a living, or who deal with foreign currency have been hard hit. Any who miss the point of government budget cuts or see entrepreneurship and investment incentives as so many big words, soon learn the truth when they buy a beer or a battleship abroad with their 'Pacific Pesos' — if they can afford it.

For the Australian dollar weakened rapidly in the 1980s. This helped make the price of Australia's mineral and farming exports more competitive but also highlighted the danger of the so-called Lucky Country becoming a Third World economy with a virtually worthless currency.

In simple terms, the downturn in the nation's economy can be blamed on a drop in world export prices for fuels, minerals, metals and primary foodstuffs which are its biggest sources of income. The price of Australia's biggest export commodity, coal — representing a quarter of its overseas trade — slumped 25 per cent in the mid 1980s. The export revenues from sugar, wheat, cotton and rice have fallen, too, and Australia faces stiff competition from subsidised producers in the United States and Europe.

Politicians and economists, armchair or professional, rant about using plentiful raw materials to cater to Australia's needs at home instead of selling these off cheaply overseas. Why should raw materials be sent overseas to be transformed and bought back as manufactured luxuries which are even more expensive and inflationary due to a weak Australian dollar? They reply to their own question by blaming pampered workers employed in flagging manufacturing industries, propped up by government tariffs, import duties and other means of industry protection which are politically expedient because they keep people in jobs.

Uncertain economic future

Yet popular economic cures like breaking the hold of unions, lowering tariffs and shifting to 'sunrise' high technology industries, or more streamlined manufacturing efforts, may be too late. Some say Australia will never return to its economic heyday of the 1950s and 1960s, for world demand for raw minerals and foodstuffs is destined to remain low. No matter how competitive Australia becomes by restructuring and boosting its manufacturers, it lags too far behind market leaders to catch up.

According to an analysis in the *Economist* in 1987: "The likely export growth is in areas of simple transformation — from bauxite to aluminium castings, for instance — when Australia can exploit its comparative advantages in minerals and cheap energies. This is not big stuff." Tourism, however, holds out much hope for Australia. Even pessimists observe that, in the long run, tourism could be more important than any gold mine to tip the balance of trade back in Australia's favour.

Since 1980, net external debt — due to loans raised by private enterprise and Australian governments — soared from $A14 billion to over $A100 billion in 1986-87. On this basis, more than a third of Australia's export earnings is needed to pay the interest alone, compared to just 8 per cent at the start of the decade. State governments have been likened to drunken sailors who spend up big on power plants, roads and other job-creating infrastructure — much of it financed by further borrowings abroad. The Federal Government deficit, despite cutbacks, was running at $A5 billion by 1986-87, again paid for by loans from abroad; Australia's international credit rating has dropped, further reflecting the fact it's been luckless of late.

Cost of living

Despite international awareness of its economic problems, Australia has no trouble raising and filling migration quotas. Outsiders believe they still have a better chance of success Down Under than elsewhere. As for those earning a living there already, dire warnings about Australia becoming a Third World economy have washed over most of them like so much warm surf.

The weakness of Australia's currency and eagerness to attract people with skills or talents to help build the economy is good news if you are thinking about spending time and money in Australia. The slump in the Australian dollar against other currencies may be advantageous for meeting the financial criteria to make the move. For the Australian dollar has still not recovered since its crash of 40 per cent against the pound sterling, 50 per cent against the Japanese yen and German mark, and 30 per cent against the US dollar in the middle 80s.

This means many immigrants who sell up homes, cars or other assets considered modest in their country of origin will increase their spending power and standard of living by moving to Australia. Despite its troubles against international currency, the buying power of the Australian dollar on its own soil remains good in relation to what you can buy for a pound in Britain, a dollar in the United States or a mark in West Germany. Interest rates are most attractive to investors at up to twice the rate of inflation in some schemes. Conversely, prime lending rates, if you need to borrow money are very high — around 20 per cent in 1987.

Unemployment

Unemployment runs at about 8 per cent, with most of Australia's long-term unemployed being either under 25, or close to retirement age: redundant or otherwise ejected from the workforce because they have no suitable skills. As detailed in Chapter 13, the Federal Government pays unemployment benefits to which most categories of permanent residents are entitled. However, the policy of sifting applicants who want to live and work in Australia is designed to avoid swelling the ranks of the jobless. Unfortunately, statistics show the risk of an immigrant being out of work in Australia was greater in the mid 1980s than 20 years ago.

In line with the long-term trend, people born outside Australia (immigrants, mostly) have a slightly higher rate of unemployment, closer to 10 per cent according to figures collated by the Australian Bureau of Statistics year after year. The greatest problem is among new Australians from non-English-speaking backgrounds. In fact, people from English-speaking countries seem to have less problem finding and keeping jobs than the average Australian, according to these figures; those from European countries like Germany and Italy have only five to six per cent unemployment in their communities Down Under, compared to a quarter to a third of refugees or unskilled migrants from Third World countries such as Vietnam or Lebanon.

4
Attitudes Down Under

Down Under, people have a way of looking at life which may not be easy for outsiders to comprehend. If, however, you plan to live and work in Australia, it is essential to know about a unique set of prejudices, stereotypes and social responses which affect the way locals see immigrant newcomers, as well as each other.

Lack of pretensions

One of the most refreshing aspects of Australian attitudes is their lack of pretensions. It's the country where a person normally sits beside and chats to a taxi driver, where the Prime Minister (Bob Hawke) appears on international television news drawling, "Owya going', mate?" to the likes of English cricketer Ian Botham. Middle Australians tend to adopt a casual, drop-in approach when socialising and working — none of this filofax-at-the-ready stuff, or effusive apologies for inconvenience which might be caused by a last-minute meeting. If it does not suit, the typical Australian will tell you straight — no airs or graces.

Money and class

It is refreshing to live in a country which is relatively classless — if class is defined by an obsession with family history, royal titles, school ties and 'old' money. New wealth will do just as nicely, thanks, and when Aussies get around to classifying people, they do so on the basis of conspicuous consumption. How many television sets do you have? Is the garage big enough to put the yacht on slips? How many exotic cars have you got in there, anyway? Where and how often can you afford to go on holiday? In short, money equals status.

Money impresses: and if you've enough of it most doors will eventually swing open. But not *all* doors. For example, the more snooty circles of rural Victoria's frightfully Anglicised 'squatocracy', or Sydney's Upper North Shore, have similar social aspirations to their predominately British ancestors. However, such preoccupations do not

22

readily filter down the social scale or even up the financial ladder in Australia — though to imply class consciousness does not exist at all Down Under would be a misrepresentation. From Perth's Peppermint Grove to Warnambool near Melbourne, from St Ives to South Yarra — and in plenty of less well-heeled enclaves too — there are those who value the 'right' school, charity balls and *entrée* to elite clubs.

Discrimination and the law
From a legal standpoint, Australia is one of the societies best-equipped to prevent and punish infringements of human rights on the basis of race, sex, colour, nationality or background. Legislation at both State and national levels makes it technically illegal in Australia to discriminate between people at work, or socially, on the basis of ethnicity, racial background, sex, sexual preference or marital status.

Homosexuals
But, if you have the idea that Australians are always in tune with the non-discriminatory, non-sexist, non-sectarian aspirations and jargon of their various State and Federal governments...forget it! The flip side of the coin is, for example, laws in Queensland which actually encourage discrimination against homosexuals and similar 'deviants'. Much has been made of this law passed in the 'Deep North' during the mid-1980s. Many were outraged by the implications of a law which enables a publican to refuse to serve a homosexual on the grounds that the person is a potential child molester.

Women
It is illegal to offer women different rates of pay for doing the same job as a man, yet female workers still average about 20 per cent lower pay. And the men themselves are not always laughing. Like women, who have Dame Edna Everage to contend with, blokes must live with internationally recognised stereotypes like Barry McKenzie and cultural attaché for the yarts, the dribbling Sir Les Patterson. True Australian chauvinists aren't joking when they say that anyone promoting the boorish 'ocker' image should have their passports withdrawn.

Migrants
Newcomers who come from other countries to live in Australia's bigger, sophisticated cities may fare better than their country cousins when it comes to fitting into society. There are many migrant and interpreter services available, and a staggering variety of ethnic social clubs, restaurants, sporting groups and other means of making contact with those of a similar origin. There's even a kind of snobbery in reverse —

people with 'natural suntans', foreign accents, or backgrounds deemed 'exotic' attract the curious admiration of the indigenous WASP (White Anglo-Saxon Protestant) majority.

But to presume that non-WASPs are welcomed with open arms everywhere they go is, unfortunately, a mistake. A glance at the section in this book on Ausslang demonstrates the fact that, Down Under, there are many unflattering terms to refer to newcomers and applied to people of ethnic background, even though they may have been in Australia all their lives. The labelling of 'New Australians' is not always 'just a joke, mate'. There are other terms for the 'wogs' far too derogatory to reproduce here — terms which it is hoped you will never hear as a foreign visitor or immigrant.

Asians

Franca Arena has lived in Australia for 30 years and is a prominent politician with wide expertise in the special problems of migrant communities. She says, "The most recent ethnic group to arrive usually bears the brunt of prejudice. For instance, when I arrived with an influx of southern Europeans, ours was the group that suffered most. Today it is the Asian community."

In Australia, the term 'Asian' refers to people of Oriental origin. Asians comprise only 2.8 per cent of the total population. More than 75 per cent of Australians are of British or Irish origin, and a fifth were born in other European countries or are of European ancestry. These days the general attitude to immigrants from Asia as well as from Europe, the Middle East and other places is more tolerant than ever before. Though you could be occasionally shocked by xenophobic prejudices or ignorance, at least you'll quickly know who your friends are. "Australians are now more reasonable, more likely to admit everyone is entitled to a 'fair go' and that it's a big country with room for all kinds. In my experience, racial problems and intolerance are far worse in the more overpopulated nations." Ms Arena observes.

Multiculturalism

Local paranoia about immigrants' impact on the status quo has largely been replaced by 'multiculturalism'. Boosted by the conviction that new blood brings with it many social, cultural and economic advantages, 'multiculturalism' means foreigners who join Australian society are not required to assimilate — in fact they are encouraged to be different and maintain traditions and languages.

According to Dr Alessandra Pucci, herself a highly successful migrant who was named Australian Businesswoman of the Year in 1985 and runs a multi-million dollar biotechnology company in Sydney, "Acceptance of foreign customs, whether in fashion, food or drink, is far greater than when I arrived here in 1970. Australian cities are far more cosmopolitan. Even Brisbane, Adelaide and smaller centres have had a shake-out due to growth and tourism.''

In Australian cities and larger towns you'll see newspaper stands groaning under the weight of 'ethnic' publications. Large, established and influential ethnic groups, such as the Italian, Greek, Asian and Eastern European communities, have a number of newspapers catering to sub-cultures within their communities, as well as their own social clubs, art galleries and museums, schools, churches and sporting organisations. Yet many migrants are shocked by the apparently informal, easy-going, even 'loose' lifestyles of the dinky-dis down the road. The real differences may not be obvious for years, emerging eventually when their children adopt local manners and values. Immigrants from places with strict social or religious codes often suffer in this clash between old ways and new. It is hardly surprising that children from non-Australian backgrounds grow up to speak with Aussie accents, take to surfing, pub-going, disco-ing and other social or sporting events considered normal for Australians but alien to their parents. A Vietnamese community leader, editor of a Vietnamese daily newspaper at Cabramatta, Sydney's suburban Saigon, summed up the problems this way: "There are some young people with multi-coloured hair, and we don't like that. In Vietnam my children never came close to me, but here they tap me on the shoulder and say: "Hello, Dad!" Sometimes this goes to extremes. I once heard a boy say to his father, "Hello, mate"!''

Australians — at Home and Overseas

"Heaven is an English policeman, a French cook, a German engineer, an Italian lover and everything organised by the Swiss.

"Hell is an English cook, a French engineer, a German policeman, a Swiss lover and everything organised by the Italians."

So says John Elliot, head of an Australian international food and drink conglomerate which, among other things, markets the Aussie beer, Fosters, around the world.

A couple of decades ago a well-travelled Aussie was the exception. Good reasons like distance, the comforts of home, plus perhaps a fear of tackling foreigners and their languages on alien turf kept Australians in Australia. But the impact of improved world communications via satellite television, imported movies and an ever more cosmopolitan urban environment has helped Aussies to lift their sunglasses to take a look around. As a result it is often easier these days to find Australians who have been to Alabama, Amsterdam and the Algarve — but not Ayers Rock.

Foreign travel is an obsession for many young Aussies. They are reputedly keen adventurers famous for making the effort to backpack it to the most unlikely, far-flung places. A grand tour 'OS' (as Australians call abroad) is a kind of finishing school: an extension of the educational process for young middle class Australians. Yet when you meet them quaffing beer in the pubs of London's Kings Road, or haggling for souvenirs in Oriental bazaars, most express supreme enthusiasm for Australia in comparison to almost any place they've been.

It is no surprise to tune into a radio chat show Down Under and hear the local xenophobes react with outrage to the notion that 'Godzone' is *not* the best country in the world with top weather/beer/fashion/food/blokes…

Blokes

When it comes to Ocker sterotypes, there are two breeds of bloke. One is naive and Neanderthal — great for a beer and a laugh. The other embodies the toughness of the adventurer — a businessbloke who conceals the dorsal fin of a shark beneath his grey suit.

The male stereotypes of Australia arise from a tough pioneering heritage: Europeans conquering an inhospitable environment, scratching out a living on outback sheep stations. The handsome image stems from the rough'n'tumble, anti-establishment attitude of convicts and outcast radicals from the 'old world,' cowboys and helmeted bushranger heroes like Ned Kelly. These were the adventurers. They pushed back the borders of the unknown by trekking, mapping and frequently dying to conquer the interior and extremities of the island continent.

Every schoolchild is taught to be proud of these aspects of Australia's 18th and 19th century colonialism, as well as the more recent legend of the Australian and New Zealand Army Corps, the ANZACS — volunteers needlessly expended in a spectacularly disastrous campaign against the Turks at Gallipoli in the First World War. Generations of novelists, playwrights, poets, painters, film-makers, cartoonists and comedians have echoed and developed that uniquely white Australian sexism embodied by the stereotypes of blokes and sheilas.

Consider the latest image of Aussie blokehood — the shark in businessman's clothing. Any suggestion that the game these blokes are playing is not quite cricket is mostly made by foreigners. At home, the entrepreneurs are greatly admired: like Alan Bond, a beer, media and yachting tycoon who brought the America's Cup to Australia and a tourist boom to Perth; or Robert Holmes à Court, originally a Rhodesian who beat the local legal and business establishment to become perhaps the richest man in Australia and a force to be reckoned with on the international business scene; football-keen John Elliot, beer and food millionaire, who also made a splash using straight Aussie tactics to snaffle desirable corporate morsels overseas.

Then there is international publisher, Rupert Murdoch, who swapped Australian citizenship for American for reasons of business rather than patriotism. But he remains dinky-di in his ruthless, no-nonsense dealings with other companies and his own employees.

Meanwhile, in a trend set by Labor Prime Minister Bob Hawke in the early 1980s, Australia's public figures make an artform of being matey and blokey when it suits them. But then, the performances of Australian politicians in various State and Federal parliamentary broadcasts, have always been exuberant. Yelling, "Get orn with it, ya Dingo!" they somehow still stay within the limits of 'parliamentary' language. A Senator in the Canberra parliament, who also happened to be a sheila, was no stranger to the cry, "Shut up you old bag!" when heckled by other honourable Senators in the chamber.

Australian males are lucky to have Paul Hogan as a role model. Known as 'Hoges', this Sydney actor constantly pops up as the thoroughly modern ocker in Australian films and television comedies. He is famous for advertising his country's beer and tourist attractions. As Mike 'Crocodile' Dundee in the highly successful movie of the same name, Hogan is naive yet shrewd, a conman with charm. Many Australians enjoy this stereotype and even seek to emulate the qualities of Paul Hogan: handsome, outdoorsy, sociable, beer-drinking, rich and famous. A self-made man and a nice bloke, too.

As in most Western nations, men tend to get together to relax. This means drinking en masse at pubs, going to the 'footy', and letting it all hang out (beer guts too) away from the prying eyes of women and children.

It would be wrong to assume a stereotype is the rule or that polarisation of the sexes is uniquely Australian. Yet anyone who has stayed awhile in an outback community would soon get a picture of the more extreme characteristics. When not utterly charming, funny and sensible, blokehood and sheiladom can be boozy, virulently racist, anti-homosexual, violent and ugly.

Sheilas

The typical Australian party is said to segregate blokes at one side of a room around the beer keg, and sheilas (also known as 'The Girls') at the other. Once again, putting too much faith in a stereotype is a mistake. A typical suburban get-together Down Under can in fact be a sundrenched, appetising and hugely sociable experience for everyone.

But once again there is more than a grain of truth in the assumption that, like the blokes, sheilas are tough. Australian women do tend to self-reliance. A suggestion by the man of the house along the lines of, "Ya don' mind chopping some wood for the barbie, do ya darls?" or the knowledge he's in the boozer with the boys *again* is part of the routine.

Like her masculine counterpart, the sheila stereotype is not always flattering. The parrakeet screech of fictitious sheilas like Barry Humphries' creation, Dame Edna Everage, is one of the least flattering aspects of the caricature, making Edna more awful to listen to than she is to look at. Humphries' 'Frankenstein' — that blue-rinsed, rhinestone-encrusted harridan — rings true for some sectors of suburban life Down Under. But *real* sheilas and their admirers are still waiting for the emergence of a sexy female stereotype to do for female egos what Paul Hogan has done for the blokes.

The modern Australian woman

These days the typical Australian woman has all the luxuries and gadgets of suburbia at her manicured finger-tips, although she's likely to be more sunbronzed, outspoken and athletic than the female stereotypes of other nations. She may not know how to operate a powersaw to chop wood for the barbie, but she'll probably not think twice about opening a door and buying her own drinks.

Many Australian men of the older as well as younger generations (who are conditioned to see male door-opening and drinks-buying as 'sexist' anyway) do not affect the kid-gloved charm of European gentlemen. In this society, blokes are not expected by their society to be old-fashioned gentlemen — and sheilas are not exactly ladies, but thoroughly modern women.

Australian women still lag behind men in terms of average pay and status at work, but the past few years have seen them gaining a grip on formerly masculine bastions like the law, business and politics. The first female High Court judge, former NSW Solicitor-General Mary Gaudron, has just been appointed. At the end of 1986, Senator Janine Haines became the first woman to lead an Australian political party when she took the top job for the Australian Democrats in Canberra.

As in Europe and America, women make the most of 'networking', to help themselves to better positions in a historically male-chauvinist society. They are entering non-traditional trades and professions; the argument is less often heard that women should stay home to give the blokes a 'fairer go.'

In the arts and media, women are well entrenched — as opera stars, authors, actresses, film directors and producers.

Politically, the women's movement has always been well advanced in Australia, indebted to Germaine Greer and compatriots. Australia was the second country in the world (after New Zealand) to give women the right to vote, in 1901. However, women did *not* gain the right to stand for Parliament until some 20 years later. These days, Australian State and Federal parliaments have one of the highest ratios of female members in the world. About one in ten MPs is a woman, a ratio only exceeded in the Scandinavian countries.

Gays

No discussion of sexual stereotypes in Australia would be complete without the role of male and female homosexuals (gays and lesbians) in society. And despite the ugliness of the term 'poofter', in the bigger cities those who have come out enjoy open and active lifestyles. But in smaller towns, rural areas and certain states, attitudes can be virulently homophobic. In Western Australia, Queensland and Tasmania sex between consenting adults of the same sex remains illegal.

In the past decade Victoria and New South Wales have repealed old laws against homosexuality, while the South Australian and Federal Governments enacted equal rights laws making discrimination on grounds of a person's sexual preferences illegal. A former premier of South Australia, Don Dunstan, actually told a television interviewer he was bisexual.

The gay community has pushed for full recognition of the non-Australian partner in a gay couple as a 'spouse' for purposes of immigration and residency applications. It is considered a step forward that, since 1983, the Federal Government has modified its rulings to give consideration on compassionate or humanitarian grounds under the immigration points system. However, the association of homosexuals with AIDS means the gay community is adopting a lower political profile.

Melbourne, Adelaide and especially Sydney have thriving gay communities. Sydney has a vibrant gay scene in the Oxford Street area, which has a population almost as high *per capita* as San Franscisco's. The Mardi Gras there each February is one of the biggest gay street festivals in the world.

Though only a minority of gays and lesbians find it possible to be quite open about their sexual preferences, the world of blokes and sheilas would not be the same without them. Homosexuals — open or otherwise — make a unique contribution to the arts, literature, academic life and entertainment in general.

Meanwhile a strong lobby seeks to show the danger of accepting homosexuality, championed by moral and relgous organisations such as the Festival of Light. The suburban and rural Australia of Bruce and Brucelene is no place for gays. There's some truth in the cliché that poofter-bashing still goes on. This is a crime which is being stamped out — but slowly. The case of a gay academic, George Duncan, allegedly murdered by police in Adelaide in 1972, led to two former policemen being charged with the killing 14 years later.

Aboriginals

The ugliest incidents of racism in Australia relate to the treatment of the aboriginal minority. It is possible to forget that the true 'first settlers' are still there at all, isolated as they usually are in outback communities or city slums. From the time of the first arrivals from Europe 200 years ago, other immigrants took it upon themselves to wipe out or supress indigenous black tribes and their culture. In country areas, shanty towns and in the cities, the condition of the 'Abos' is often pathetic, and presents an unpleasant example of progress-gone-haywire.

Australia has even been labelled the 'South Africa' of the Pacific. Supporters of this point of view describe white Australians as passive racists, only saved from being cast into the apartheid camp by the fact that whites are now in the majority. The Aboriginals and Torres Strait Islanders number about 160,000 or 1 per cent of the population.

Respectable white society is embarrassed at the ill-treatment of the black minority by the police and other whites. Yet it is not unusual to hear such discrimination condoned — even by otherwise worldly, well-educated members of migrant minority groups who have, ironically, been victims of discrimination themselves. Their conventional wisdom is that the Abos are a drunken, lazy, useless lot quite beyond help and redemption.

At last an effort is being made to apply multiculturalism to Aboriginals, too. Many white Australians identify with the sound of the didgeridoo (an Aboriginal wind instrument), native dances, native bark and rock paintings of nature, myths of the Dreamtime and other aspects of an isolated Stone Age culture unchanged for thousands of years and well suited to the bush and desert environments of the island continent.

The Dreamtime

Aboriginal culture is based on the Dreamtime philosophy, giving spiritual focus to the land, and fusing past, present and future. It is believed that the peoples now known as Australian Aboriginals and Torres Strait Islanders crossed from South-East Asia more than 50,000 years ago, and that the natives numbered anywhere from 300,000 to 1 million when the European invasion started in earnest in 1788.

Oppression of the Aborigines

Apart from slaughtering the blacks like wild animals and exploiting them mercilessly, the British settlers infected them with hitherto unknown diseases and introduced the natives to the corrupting influence of alchohol. In Tasmania, Aboriginals were massacred to the point of extinction. Today about half the remaining Aboriginal population lives in the cities, surviving largely on government handouts in reserved areas or elsewhere.

The guilty conscience of the white Australian community is such that it agrees to subsidise Aboriginals to the tune of 70 per cent of this minority group's total income. Freehold ownership of some 10 per cent of Australia's land mass has been returned to the natives, and many tribes are paid royalties as a result. Ayers Rock, that huge red boulder in the desert of the Northern Territory, is the most famous of the sites returned to the Aboriginals in the mid-1980s by a progressive Labor administration in Canberra after decades of agitation by white and black activists in the name of Aboriginal rights.

In Western Australia Ernie Bridge became the first Aboriginal to be appointed as a Cabinet Minister by the State Government in 1986, though a number of Aboriginals have been parliamentarians in Australia before him.

The plight of black Australians is reflected in recent figures showing they are more than ten times more likely than other Australians to have served a prison sentence (some 726.5 per 100,000 compared to 60 of every 100,000 whites). Aboriginal rights activists claim this is proof of widespread police harassment, exemplified by a Queensland case in which an Aboriginal was jailed for three months for stealing two loaves of bread. On the other hand, the Court of Criminal Appeal in 1986 noted a tendency for judges to treat Aboriginals more leniently than other offenders.

Despite the principle that Australians of all races should enjoy equal legal rights, statistics show the indigenous blacks are far from equal in an otherwise affluent, sophisticated society. Alcohol abuse drags down many members of the older generation while petrol sniffing is common among youngsters. Unemployment is about three times that of whites; infant mortality and disease is rife compared to other social groups while the average life expectancy for an Aboriginal is around 52 years, some 20 years less than the national average (The *Times*, London, 1986).

In recent years more subtle means have been devised by governments to encourage Aborigines to improve their circumstances. For instance, instead of paying millions in what Aboriginals call 'sit-down money' to their army of unemployed, the Federal Government is channelling money to Aboriginal communities for self-help projects.

5
Going to Australia —
How Will You Get In?

Many people misunderstand the Australian rules and regulations which govern permanent and temporary stays there. They assume the rules exist to keep people OUT. The truth, however, is that in the past few years these rules have been reviewed, altered and interpreted with a view to letting the 'right' people IN.

This Chapter aims to explain how Australia's quite complex system of categories, concessions and accumulation of 'points' works, so you can judge the chances for the success of your own application. What's more, the price you pay for this book will be far less than the cost of a wasted fee, which you must pay in order to have your application processed in many circumstances (see section of **Fees** below). Fees are payable on lodging an application and, if you are rejected, you will have nothing to show for your money.

A more relaxed policy

Australia has substantially relaxed its migration policy in recent years. Its aim is to be more open to people likely to make a good life there — both for the benefit of the newcomer and the nation. Whether you have relatives in Australia already, a little money or lots of it, whether you want to study or take a working holiday, an offer of a job or not, Australia's rules on entry are more flexible now than ever before. For your application, plans for a stay in Australia should fall into one of the following categories:

- **A holiday visit.** No intention of working — just a trip abroad, perhaps with an eye open for business, work, educational or lifestyle opportunities for yourself or your family back home.

- **A working holiday.** A temporary stay presents chances to gain work experience, live in a fresh environment, make money for holidaying while in Australia and on your way to and from there.

- **Educational purposes.** Australia's educational institutions may well provide equivalent or better opportunities for study than in other places; you'd also have the excitement and experience of living in a new place.

- **Temporary residence.** Your plan might be to take a short-term job in your field of expertise, either brought in by an Australian company or educational institution, or posted there by employers in your home country.

- **Permanent residence.** A long-term commitment to the ideal of living and working in Australia. You may have friends or family you want to join; you may want to retire in a sunny, untroubled environment; you may decide Australia is a fine place for your own career to flourish and for your children to grow up.

Additionally, Australia's entry rules will make it possible for people to settle there for **humanitarian** reasons, often because they are aged, ill or as refugees from a regime or government at home which presents a serious threat to their welfare.

Illegal immigrants

Overriding the rules and regulations is the law in Australia on illegal immigrants and people working without permits. Since many more people want to live there than Australia can accommodate, the law regarding people who overstay their visas, or who are found to be working in contravention of the terms of their (eg visitor) visas, is tough. There are about 60,000 illegal immigrants in Australia, according to estimates published in 1987. People of British origin represent the biggest single group of illegal migrants in Australia. Such people face either virtual 'imprisonment' in the country, since they would probably be detected if they tried to leave, or deportation and a heavy fine if they are discovered. The illegal migrant also faces deprivation of the privilege to make future visits for at least five years — if at all. The Australian Government has not declared an amnesty on illegal migrants (meaning they can come forward and stay on, if they like) since the early 1980s and it now requires a special Act of the Federal Parliament to declare amnesties in future.

Visitors who inadvertently overstay their visas should contact the Department of Immigration to sort out their problems.

External application

The other important point to bear in mind, if you are thinking of going to Australia temporarily (perhaps with a mind to becoming a permanent settler later) is that your application for migration must be made from *outside* the country. Normally, you may *not* apply for permanent residence while in Australia.

Application fees

You can expect to pay a fee, sometimes substantial, on application for some visas, work permits or immigration papers. Fees are also charged for citizenship applications made once a person has settled in Australia. The aim is to ensure that applicants for entry to Australia are serious in their intentions, and that the Australian authorities are not wasting precious bureaucratic resources processing half-hearted applications. You will *not* normally have access to counselling by Australia's migration or visa officials when you apply. So, if you do not plan your application carefully, it could be rejected and you would have wasted money paid in fees, which are not refundable.

Fees for visas can be paid in the currency of a foreign country, equivalent to the amount of Australian dollars being charged for the visa. These charges alter with time but, as a guide, the rates shown in the box (in Australian dollars) applied in 1987:

Application Fees

— sponsorship for temporary residents $A145
— application for further temporary
    entry permit (extension) $A35
— application for permission to work
    (lodged in Australia) $A60
— application for change of status
    to permanent resident $A200
— application for migration to Australia
    — on lodgement $A60
— application for migration to Australia
    — on final processing $A165
— application for new resident return
    visa (lodged in Australia) $A50
— application for new resident return
    visa (lodged overseas) $A60
— application for evidence of resident
    status $A50
— application for registration of Australian
    citizenship by descent $A50
— application for Declaratory Certificate
    of Australian Citizenship $A30

Health and character checks

Everyone who applies to visit, take temporary work or to settle in Australia permanently is subject to health and character checks. An applicant and his or her dependants planning to enter under the same visa must undergo **medical examinations** to prove they are in sound health. **Criminal records** may also be checked by Australian migration and visa authorities to ensure the people being granted a visa are of good character.

There is some flexibility in the way Australia's 'good health and character' rules are implemented. For example, elderly people with their only close relatives in Australia may be allowed entry although they are chronically ill, while minor criminal offences may be discounted, if the applicant has a good case otherwise to go to Australia.

Age limits

In many circumstances age limits also apply, as in applications for a temporary residence visa for a working holiday and many categories of permanent residence applications.

VISITOR VISAS

Visitor visas are free of charge. They are normally issued for six months or less for purposes such as

- tourism
- business (negotiations or discussions — though not for taking up employment)
- seeing relatives or friends
- pre-arranged medical treatment
- for academics taking up to twelve months' sabbatical leave at an Australian institution

This is the entry visa you will probably require for an initial look at Australia — the people, their lifestyle, a range of vastly differing climates and locations, as well as opportunities for career, business, or investment should you decide to apply for migration or temporary residence at a later stage.

The visitor visa application form, available from the nearest Australian embassy or high commission, must be completed and returned with a passport-type photograph and a valid passport.

The Australian Government does not require visitors to be sponsored. However, some countries do require the would-be traveller to Australia to be sponsored by a friend or relative they propose to visit there. An important proviso for obtaining a visitor visa is that the applicant should not intend to take a job in Australia or start formal studies. If the holder of a visitor visa is discovered to be working or studying illegally, they will be fined (up to $A1,000, at the time of writing) and told to leave.

Extensions
Extensions of the visitor visa may be granted under certain circumstances to people who make the application before their first visitor visa has expired, though stays totalling more than six months are not normally allowed. However, visiting academics and aged relatives of Australian citizens may be allowed to stay in the country under such a visa for up to twelve months.

Multiple entry
Multiple entry visas may be issued to people who can show good reasons for coming to and going from Australia quite frequently — parents with children living there, business visitors, or people planning to interrupt their stay in Australia to travel to another country and then resume their visit to Australia.

Medical treatment
Those wanting a visitor visa for **medical treatment** in Australia must meet a range of requirements. They must convince visa officials

- that they can meet the costs of that medical treatment
- that satisfactory arrangements have been made for this with Australian hospital/medical specialists in advance
- that such treatment is not available in their own country
- that they will receive significant benefit from such a short term of treatment in Australia
- that they will *not* pose a public health risk (because they have a contagious disease, for example)

People staying less than six months who are not from countries with reciprocal arrangements with Australia for health insurance (see Chapter 13) will need private or travel insurance to cover possible medical expenses in Australia. Hospitals and medical care in Australia — whether public or private — can be extremely expensive.

TEMPORARY RESIDENT VISAS

This type of visa covers a range of applicants and their families who want to come to Australia to live, work or study for short periods. While the principal applicant may be granted permission to take a job in Australia, a spouse or other family member coming with that person is not usually allowed to take a job.

Sponsors

The concept of the **sponsor** is important for many types of applicants for temporary residence. The sponsor must be an Australian resident and

- an **individual**
- or in some cases a **company**, religious, educational or sporting **institution**

willing to take financial and legal responsibility for the temporary resident. The sponsor must be prepared to guarantee the entrant's income while in Australia, and guarantee that the proposed job, if any, is within the terms of relevant employment awards (wages and conditions) in Australia. A sponsor is also responsible for the entrant's welfare, housing, and must pay an application fee.

WORKING HOLIDAYMAKERS

Unlike most other categories of temporary residents, people allowed to take working holidays in Australia do *not* need a sponsor.

Working holiday applicants must be

- between 18 and 25 years old, preferably, or under 30 in certain cases
- single, or couples without children

The goal is to promote international understanding by allowing young people to live and work for short periods in foreign countries. The money earned on the strength of such a work permit is meant to help finance more travel around Australia. The job done to earn the money is supposed to be an 'incidental' of the total adventure, *not* a career move. Since youth unemployment is quite high in Australia, people who enter under this category must not be perceived as a threat to the job opportunities of Australians.

Australia has working holiday arrangements with the following countries:

- Britain   — The Netherlands
- The Republic of Ireland   — Japan
- Canada

Nationals of all these countries except Japan may apply for working holiday permits from any foreign country, including their own. Japanese applicants must apply for the necessary visa from Japan only. Applicants from other countries whose entry is considered of mutual advantage as a worthwhile cultural exchange and who are applying in their countries of citizenship may also be considered for places under the working holiday scheme. They must also be seen as self-reliant, resourceful and adaptable, by the Australian authorities.

To qualify applicants must:

- state their prime intention is a **holiday** in Australia, with paid employment as an incidental aspect

- have a **return ticket,** or enough money to buy one

- have **reasonable funds** for normal living whether they are in a paid job or not, at least during the first weeks of their holiday and perhaps while looking for work. Australian authorities in your country can advise on how much money is considered 'reasonable' when you apply, dependent on factors such as whether you have friends or relatives to stay with in your travels, how much money would be left after paying for a return ticket and so forth

- have fair prospects of obtaining **temporary employment** to supplement the holiday funds taken to Australia for holiday purposes

- *not* be responding to any **organised attempt at labour market recruitment** by an agency or employer. A pre-arranged job is only acceptable if it is the result of the personal initiative of the applicant

- sign a **declaration** not to undertake any studies in Australia, apart from a short-term English language course

- be **aged 18 to 25, single,** or **married couples without children**. An applicant aged 26 to 30 may apply in the home country, if they are citizens of one of the arrangement countries listed above and provided their entry would be considered of mutual advantage

Only one such permit for a working holiday in Australia is allowed — once you have been there under this provision, you cannot apply for a second such stay.

Mutual advantage is open to interpretation by officials in charge of such temporary visas at the time. It means simply that the applicant is likely to gain 'cultural understanding' through the working holiday Down Under. If that means they get to know the difference between a Hunter claret and a Coonawarra hermitage, so much the better. Most people of good health and character (no criminal offences) are admitted under these terms to see something of Australia while they are young and free.

However, if you are demonstrably unable to support yourself for a short time in Australia — under the stipulation that an applicant have 'reasonable funds' explained above — you will probably be refused a visa.

Professional qualifications

You may have professional qualifications which you hope to use while in Australia on a working holiday. Assuming the visa authorities are satisfied that work and career are *not* your main considerations in applying for a working holiday permit, your qualifications may first have to be assessed by Australia's Commission on Overseas Professional Qualifications (see Chapter 6) which can take weeks, even months. An interview may also be necessary

- for applicants older than 25
- if the intended stay in Australia is longer than six months
- if the application is made outside that person's country of citizenship
- or if Australia's visa officials decide it is desirable for some other reason

The three month rule

Working holidaymakers are not allowed to stay in the same full-time job longer than three months. Anyone who does so will not be allowed a further entry permit to Australia.

English courses

Working holidaymakers may enrol in full-time, single English courses which are not more than ten weeks in duration. Part-time English courses may be taken, provided this remains an 'incidental activity' to the holiday stay in Australia. English study can only be undertaken at accredited English language institutions (those offering English language as a subject).

Six-month stay

Six months is the usual time allowed for working holiday visas. Extensions may be allowed to people with a good case to stay on (like needing time to arrange the rest of their foreign travel) and who show they have abided by the terms of the scheme so far. Extensions beyond a total period of 12 months are not allowed.

EXECUTIVE, TECHNICAL AND PROFESSIONAL STAFF FOR COMPANIES IN AUSTRALIA

Sponsorship by the prospective employer is not necessary for people seeking permission to stay in Australia for four months or less. In the case of senior executive and specialist staff, the application for temporary residence may be approved if a detailed case is made showing a need for such experts in Australia by

- either the prospective Australian employer
- or the person's usual employer overseas, with a branch in Australia where it is hoped to post that employee.

Four years maximum
Applications for the temporay residence of such an expert and his or her family are normally granted for periods of up to four years, provided:

— the proposed employer provides **sponsorship** and pays the fee
— labour market testing in Australia shows the **required skills** are not available there
— the position is **full-time**
— the applicant for the visa will **not be underpaid** in terms of Australia's industrial awards (pay and conditions)
— foreigners are **not being brought in as a substitute for training** of Australians for certain jobs, and the employer may be required to introduce training schemes for local staff
— the applicant is not being recruited to fill an **unskilled** or **semi-skilled** job
— **health and character** requirements are met.

STAFF FOR AUSTRALIAN EDUCATIONAL AND RESEARCH INSTITUTIONS

If the applicant is seen to provide enrichment of Australia's educational environment, as well as an awareness of other cultures, the rules permit entry of academic staff for temporary postings. If they plan to stay four months or less they may be approved without sponsorship, as long as they show evidence of their engagement by an Australian educational institution or organisation. Sponsorship by the proposing academic institutions is necessary for applications for stays longer than four months. The proposed post must be relevant to their qualifications and experience.

Junior academic and non-academic staff

These may apply and be approved for entry of longer than four months if:

- labour market testing shows the **required skills** are not available within the existing Australian workforce
- acceptable **sponsorship**, accompanied by the prescribed fee, is lodged by the proposed employer
- the **pay and conditions** are consistent with Australian industrial awards
- **health and character** requirements are met

Senior academic staff

Staff at lecturer level and above may be approved subject to the requirements listed above for junior staff. However, sponsoring institutions need not show they have searched the local labour market to find someone to fill the particular position. It is accepted by the visa authorities that this has already been done, and the best person for the post (ie the applicant) has been chosen.

Applications from senior academic and post-doctoral research staff may be approved for up to **four years'** temporary residence in Australia. **Extensions** may be granted, as long as the appointees stay with the academic institution or organisation which sponsored them in the first place.

SPORTSPEOPLE AND ASSOCIATED PERSONNEL

In sports-mad Australia, this category of temporary residence aims to encourage sporting contacts with stars from abroad to improve sporting standards in Australia. Applicants wanting to come to Australia for less than four months do not need a sponsor if they are coming to participate in specific events or contests, provided:

- they show evidence of an **invitation** from the organisers of the event or evidence of acceptance of a nomination to participate in an event open to contestants from overseas
- they sign a declaration that on arrival in Australia they will have a **return or onward ticket** and **sufficient funds** to support themselves (and family members travelling with them) for the duration of the proposed stay.

Show or competition judges entering for less than four months do not require sponsorship.

Stays over four months
Applicants wanting to stay longer than four months to participate in specific events or contests:

- need a **sponsor** to pay the relevant fee and lodge the application in Australia
- must envisage a stay of no longer than **twelve months**

Persons and teams of international standing and their personnel do not need sponsorship, and may apply directly to Australian embassies and high commissions for temporary entry to Australia.

ENTERTAINERS

Entertainers or other professional workers in entertainment industries with **special talents or abilities** may be allowed to enter Australia to work for a limited period. An acceptable sponsorship must be lodged by a reputable organisation in Australia.

RELIGIOUS STAFF

People seeking visas to engage in religious duties on a temporary basis must be sponsored by an established religious organisation in Australia.

CONDITIONS OF TEMPORARY VISAS

Apart from the conditions described above, people who suceed in their application for a temporary residence visa are not allowed to change *either* their jobs *or* their sponsors after they arrive. For stays of longer than twelve months, or where the person would be entering a classroom situation as a result of the job, applicants must undertake a **medical and radiological examination** before the visa is issued.

Those in Australia for less than six months should have **private health insurance** during their stay, since medical and hospital care — public or private — can be expensive. Australia's national health scheme (**Medicare**) does not cover people who stay less than six months, unless the applicant's country of citizenship has a reciprocal health agreement with Australia (see Chapter on **Australian Health and Welfare**).

IMMIGRATION CATEGORIES — HOW DO YOU GET IN?

Australia has a range of rules and regulations for people intending to become permanent residents, which should be considered before lodging your application and fee. Nobody wants to waste time, emotional energy and money in useless effort banging on Australia's door. No matter how much you may want to go to Australia, **first consider why Australia would want you**...for such is the main consideration of people who make the decisions on immigration applications.

The migration officers at Australia's embassies and high commissions around the world are well trained, flexible and often sympathetic — but an appliction may be knocked back long before it reaches the **interview stage** (if any), so you may never benefit from counselling. What follows is not a do-it-yourself kit to **migration counselling**, though it may open your eyes to the possibility of fitting the bill for one category better than others. Then tailor your application accordingly and seek advice from an Australian migration officer, if possible, or the Department of Immigration and Ethnic Affairs which is in charge of such matters. The health and character considerations already mentioned are especially relevant for people who want to become permanent residents, though as stated previously, there is some flexibility in interpretation for humanitarian reasons.

Most applicants will need either a close relative who can sponsor them for migration or the skills, finance and personal qualities to contribute to society and the economy.

FAMILY MIGRATION

Of all the migration categories, family reunion has been and remains the biggest source of newcomers to Australia — accounting for about a third of successful applicants. The **Points Test**, which certain applicants for migration need to pass in order to gain permission to go to Australia, does *not* apply. To qualify as a family migrant you must be sponsored by:

- a spouse
- a son or daughter under 18 and dependant members of the family unit
- a parent, if you are under 18 years old
- a fiancé(e)

Sponsors

Relatives who sponsor applicants must pay the relevant fee and lodge the *Sponsorship for Migration to Australia* form, must be at least 18 years old and either Australian citizens or permanent residents of the country (ie someone who has gone there as a migrant).

The sponsorship form must include **original or certified copies of documents** proving the sponsor's relationship to the applicant for migration, and of the sponsor's Australian citizenship (if he or she is an Australian citizen).The sponsor must

- provide the information and advice you need to settle into your new life in Australia
- ensure adequate housing is available on arrival and, if necessary, provide accommodation for you in the first 12 months
- provide financial assistance to meet your living expenses in the first twelve months, if necessary

The capacity of that sponsoring relative to meet financial and housing requirements may be checked by Australian immigration officials.

Assurance of support
If you, as an applicant, are of working age your sponsor may also be required to provide a job. If you are the mother (aged 50 or over) or father (aged 55 or over) of your sponsor in Australia, your relative must sign an **Assurance of Support**. This document makes the sponsoring relative *liable to repay* any social security benefits (see Chapter 13 on **Health and Welfare**, for immigrant entitlements) which may be paid to you by the Government or by a charity for the first ten years, unless you acquire Australian citizenship in the meantime. Your sponsor will not have to repay the money after you have become a citizen.

Submission of form
After the sponsor has filled in the *Sponsorship for Migration* form, it must be sent to you (the applicant) with any supporting documents and a number of forms to be completed and returned to the nearest Australian migration office at a high commission or embassy.

Eligibility of family and relatives
The table on the opposite page summarises the eligibility of family members and relatives to accompany the applicant.

SKILLED LABOUR AND BUSINESS MIGRATION

This category covers a number of opportunities prospective immigrants can use to gain permission to work in Australia as permanent residents. A **Points Test**, relevant for certain immigrant applicants, does *not* apply to people in this category. It is possible to gain a visa in this category if it is accepted that you fill one of these criteria:

- The Occupational Share System
- The Employer Nomination Scheme
- The Business Migration Programme

Eligibility of family and relatives

Spouses
Approval for migration is not automatic, and spouses must first be assessed for good health and character.

Children
If unmarried and still part of the sponsor's family unit, they must first be assessed for good health and character. If older than 18 and independent, see the Independent and Concessional Category.

Parents
If of or older than the retirement age in Australia (60 for women, 65 for men) sponsored parents are assessed for good health and character. Objections on medical grounds are common in such cases; these will be dismissed in most cases by the Australian migration authorities unless the person has a catastrophic disability (permanently hospitalised or having communicable diseases). An *Assurance of Support* from the sponsor is also required, and their chances of settling into life in Australia satisfactorily are taken into account. If the sponsored parents are of working age and they are assessed to have a good chance of a happy settlement in Australia, the sponsor must pre-arrange employment, in some cases, the sponsor's *Assurance of Support* will also be necessary.

Fiancés
Fiancés are admitted at first on a temporary basis for three months. Proof of a genuine marriage will make them eligible for permanent residence. A fiancé must be known to the sponsor, not just coming to Australia for an arranged marriage; they must have a real intention to marry. They are assessed for good health and character. The sponsor must provide evidence from an authorised marriage celebrant that the marriage will take place three months after the fiancé's arrival in Australia.

Special Applicants
Family reunion provisions may also be extended for cases like children for adoption, certain orphans, relatives required to help overcome a serious family crisis such as death or a prolonged illness, and wholly supported relatives over retirement age. There are also concessions for brothers, sisters, and non-dependant children who are the last family members living outside Australia.

The Occupational Share System (OSS)

There are occasional vacancies for skilled workers from overseas which cannot be filled by the labour market in Australia. After applicants from Australia have been sought and found wanting, employers may notify State or Federal Governments that there is a shortage in a particular field. Each July a survey results in an updated list (reviewed each December); this shows the occupations needing foreign recruits as part of the drive to attract the most usefully qualified migrants to fill the gaps. A number of **shares** are allocated for each occupation, indicating how many people are needed to fill available jobs. When all shares have been used up (ie positions filled) that occupation is removed from the list.

Applicants for jobs in **trades** must have completed a period of formal training qualifying them to work in that trade in their own country, and should also have worked in that trade for at least five years. **Professional** applicants should have qualifications acceptable in Australia, through its Commission on Overseas Professional Qualifications, plus three to five years' post-graduate experience.

Since the list of defined trades or professions in the OSS changes at least once a year, it is best to ask for the latest list from the nearest Australian embassy or high commission. In recent years a range of work — from skilled waiters, motor mechanics, nurses and school teachers to economists, actuaries and physiotherapists — has been on the list. To be eligible to migrate under OSS, you must be under 45 years old. The dependant children and spouse of each applicant must also be of good health and character, as well as satisfying general criteria in convincing migration authorities the individual/family will make a successful transition to life in Australia.

Employer Nomination Scheme (ENS)

People under the age of 55 may be nominated under this scheme by an Australian employer for a specific job. The ENS is designed to enable Australian employers to recruit highly skilled workers from overseas when they have been unable to fill the vacancies through the domestic job market or through their own training efforts.

If and when employment nomination is approved in Australia by the Department of Immigration and Ethnic Affairs, the nearest migration office to the nominated worker will contact that person, who will then be invited to apply formally. Australian employers needing certain expertise they believe cannot be provided in Australia may advertise in the foreign press — professional or trade journals, perhaps. Or you may discover the shortage in your field personally, during a holiday or business visit to Australia, and start your application process through contacts you make while there, though the application should be lodged by you in your home country.

At the time of writing, employers were seeking immigrant employees with skills and experience as

- cabinet makers
- computer sales persons
- physiotherapists
- toolmakers
- upholsterers and machinists

among others. However, the list of occupations in demand changes from time to time, and only one job may exist within a particular job category!

As with the OSS described above, the applicant must be able to show proof of gaining qualifications which are acceptable to Australian authorities, as well as work experience.

Business Migration Programme (BMP)

A whole chapter of this book is devoted to this broad-ranging and flexible category. Australia places increasing emphasis on it, declaring an interest in attracting immigrants who are likely to be self-employed and self-made. Broadly, they should apply as businesspeople with:

- a **business investment** of at least $A500,000 to offer if they go to live and work in Australia, or
- **entrepreneurial abilities**, a joint venture proposed with a company already in business in Australia, high technology proposals of benefit to Australia, provided they have adequate funds and appropriate experience.

Applicants and members of their family they want to take with them must fill the general criteria like good health and character required by immigration authorities. For details on BMP, see Chapter 7.

INDEPENDENT AND CONCESSIONAL MIGRATION

This is the only category for which the **Points Test** applies. Like any test or examination, the applicant is given a certain number of points for his or her different qualities as a prospective migrant. It is necessary to obtain 70 points to 'pass' the test for issue of a permanent residence visa to settle in Australia.

'Independent and Concessional' is a relatively new grouping for migrants, and gives some weight (through allocation of extra points) to people with relatives already living in Australia as permanent residents.

If the sponsors are also Australian citizens, more points are scored by the applicant. Brothers, sisters, non-dependant children, nephews and nieces may be sponsored by relatives in Australia. Applicants are expected to buy and lodge sponsorship forms in the way explained in the **family reunion** section. Other fees for migration application also apply.

People without family sponsors can apply directly to the nearest Australian embassy or high commission. If you are an 'independent' applicant (with no relatives to sponsor you) it is possible to score extra points in other areas; you may 'pass' and be assessed as suitable for migration whether you have relatives in Australia already or not. The categories under which points are scored cover:

- concessional points for existence of a sponsoring relative
- employability
- skills
- education
- age

Occupations

You do not have to be in any specific occupational group, though will be given more points if you show you could fill a gap in the workforce, according to updated lists referred to by the immigration officials. At the time of writing, the occupations listed included

- hairdresser
- bricklayer
- offset printer
- petroleum engineer
- stenographer/secretary
- journalist and subeditor

Work experience, a sound continuous employment record or employment arranged by a sponsor (the relative) also scores points. If you do not need to be retrained or take an English language course to make you employable in Australia, points are scored. However, even people with a sound employment record requiring limited language training may score points.

Education and age

A recognised tertiary qualification (from a university, or post-secondary college) and the ability to speak and write English fluently are highly desirable, adding to the points accumulated by the applicant. But even completing a degree course is unnecessary; points are allocated for completion of full secondary education (at least 12 years' schooling) or part secondary education (at least 8 years' schooling).

'Mature young people' (between 18 and 35) are given the most points in the age-score, though if you are 35 to 44 at the time of assessment, some points will also be given, though none are allocated to applicants aged 45 or over.

SELF-SUPPORTING RETIREES AND OTHERS

People who wish to retire to Australia but without children living there are considered if they have reached the age of 55, and meet certain financial requirements as well as being of good health and character.

If considering migrating under this category, bear in mind that you will *not* be able to make free use of Australia's public health and welfare facilities because you will *not* have contributed to Australia's development by paying taxes during your working life.

Assets

On retiring to Australia, applicants are therefore expected to have enough money *not* to become a burden on the Australian community. Under new capital requirements introduced in 1987, they'll need to be rather wealthy by Australian standards. To qualify as a self-supporting retiree, you will need $A500,000 to transfer to Australia, to cover what migration authorities call 'establishment costs': buying a house, cars, private health insurance and anything else needed in daily life. This would also leave the retiree with enough capital to invest to generate a good income.

Or the applicant must have $A150,000 for establishment costs, plus a pension or other capital for investment to provide an annual income of $A35,000 for married couples, and $A30,000 for single applicants. Such amounts are well above the average annual income in Australia, at around $A22,000 a year in 1987.

Applications by intending migrants in this category must include comprehensive details and evidence of their claimed financial position.

Other self-supporting applicants

Some people may find they stand a good chance of permanent residence in Australia if they are:

- **former Australian citizens** who have maintained ties with the country but lost their citizenship by acquiring that of another country for 'good' reasons
- people who spent their **formative years** in Australia and have maintained ties there
- people with a **record of achievement** in creative or sporting fields, which would benefit Australia
- people not eligible under other categories but who have **outstanding characteristics** which would be of benefit to Australia
- **refugees**, displaced persons and other applicants allowed into Australia on humanitarian grounds. This has been an important category for the entry of thousands of refugees, mostly from South-East Asia. As this region continues to become more politically stable, the number of refugees and displaced persons allowed to come from there to Australia on humanitarian grounds is expected to drop. Since Australia is committed to such humanitarian and refugee programmes, wars and conflicts elsewhere may again increase the number of refugees coming into Australia.

PROCESSING APPLICATIONS

How long does it take?

The time taken by different migration offices to process an immigration application is variable. In places where there is no Australian migration office, you must send your application to a nearby nation and even travel there for interviews.

Since the middle 1980s cutbacks in staff numbers at Australian immigration offices around the world means personal interviews and counselling facilities are the exception rather than the rule. So be prepared with full documentation and other evidence to enclose with your application papers so your case can be assessed as efficiently as possible; avoid delays due to unnecessary letter writing and requests for further information, valid certificates, accountants' statements or anything else the Australian government needs to decide your eligibility.

At the time of writing, the authorities suggested about three months as the average time you can expect for approval (or otherwise) of your application, if in the family reunion category. It takes about eight months in most other categories. There may be extra delays due to the time needed to arrange a job in Australia in advance (if this is relevant to the application), checks on health and character, and absence of documentary evidence of employment and training.

Therefore, decide whether you really *want* to go, *know* what you are getting into if your application is accepted, and be prepared to organise your own counselling — ie study the rest of this book and bone up on Australia generally!

Getting help

State and non-government ethnic advisory councils and services are available in the big cities, and able to give advice suited to your circumstances and plans both before you finalise an application and, if successful, after you start living in Australia. For factual information, contacting relevant trade unions, ethnic communities and professional/educational/business organisations in Australia may be useful, and of course friends or relatives already living there are invaluable sources of information and advice.

Government trade officials, State houses or their representatives around the world may provide some counselling and help with research and planning for the move, as indicated elsewhere.

TO-ING AND FRO-ING

If and when your application for permanent residence as an immigrant to Australia is successful, you will be issued a **resident return visa** along with your **migrant visa.**

On entering Australia on the migrant visa, the resident return visa comes into force. It is normally valid for three years. This is a considerable relaxation of past rules when — except for special business or humanitarian reasons — immigrants were expected to stay at least a year to show they were serious about settlement.

The issue of these multiple re-entry visas to newcomers became automatic on 1st January 1987, though people who had migrated to

Australia at any time before that may apply.

The resident return visa allows the bearer to enter and re-enter the country any number of times — a right normally accorded only to people with Australian passports. The freedom to come and go as you please in the first three years of settlement is useful for people starting or transferring their business ventures to Australia, selling or moving financial assets abroad, wanting to see friends and relatives in their country of origin, or to go back simply because they are homesick.

However, the Australian migration authorities will not be happy to renew a resident return visa if the bearer has been to-ing and fro-ing to such an extent he or she has been out of the country for more than one year of the first three. But there is some flexibility in these regulations and the authorities will consider whether the individual had good personal or business reasons for remaining outside the country for long periods.

Appeals

If your application for renewal of your resident return visa is refused, appeals can be made through the **Immigration Review Panel**.

Finally

Of course, those who become Australian citizens (see below) after migrating to Australia will not need to renew their resident return visa each time they take a trip overseas and want to re-enter Australia. New Zealand passport holders do not need a special re-entry visa either, in order to enter Australia.

AUSTRALIAN CITIZENSHIP

You may be wanting to certify your Australian descent or citizenship in order to live there — while everyone who migrates may one day decide to take the option of becoming Australian citizens to confirm their loyalty to their adopted country. However, the move to citizenship is quite a separate matter from gaining permission to move there as a *permanent resident*, the initial status for most migrants. There is no pressure on you to take Australian citizenship if it does not suit you — since often you will be required to give up previous citizenship rights. However, there are clear advantages — and duties — in becoming a citizen of Australia. Anyone who has lived in Australia as a permanent resident more than two years can apply. Before looking at the rules, consider what Australian citizenship entails. In contrast to permanent residents, *Australian citizens:*

- can take out an Australian **passport**
- can **re-enter** Australia from abroad without permission or visas
- may **stand for election** to State or Federal parliaments
- **must vote.** They are fined if registered on an electoral roll but fail to cast a vote in person or by postal ballot at State and Federal elections, unless electoral officers are satisfied with the reason why that citizen could not fulfil this duty
- may be employed permanently in the **government public service** (unless that person is a British citizen, as is still the case in some States of Australia, when the job applicant has the same rights as an Australian citizen)
- can apply for **full welfare benefits**, without obligation to repay them in full, as is the case for some migrants who have been sponsored by relatives or others undertaking to support them if/when they are unable to work. As detailed in the Chapter on **Australian Health and Welfare,** sponsors may be liable to repay any welfare benefits claimed by permanent residents.

Deportation
A resident who is *not* a citizen may also be deported if:

- he/she has been convicted of any offence within ten years of arriving in Australia and is sentenced to jail for a year or more
- has lived in Australia less than ten years and the Minister for Immigration and Ethnic Affairs decides that person is a threat to the national security.

Appeals against deportation orders may be made to the Administrative Appeals Tribunal, the Federal Court or the High Court. The Federal Government Ombudsman may also be able to consider the case and advise on chances of a successful appeal.

Pledge of allegiance
Citizenship, and a certificate to state the person's new nationality, is granted at a formal ceremony in which people are required to pledge allegiance to Australia. A fee must be paid for the issue of such a certificate (see section on **Fees** in this Chapter) to cover processing of the application.

To apply, a permanent resident must have spent two years living in Australia out of the previous five years, excluding any time they were outside the country for business trips, holidays etc. Technically the rules are that a permanent resident qualifying for citizenship must have spent:

- two years in Australia out of the previous five years
- twelve months in the two years immediately prior to the application in Australia.

LOSING AND RENOUNCING AUSTRALIAN CITIZENSHIP

Australians who have applied for or been born to Australian citizenship may also lose this status, its rights and privileges under special circumstances. If they take the citizenship of another country (other than automatically, such as by birth or marriage), Australians may have this citizenship withdrawn. It does not matter where they live on acquiring the other citizenship. On the other hand, a person marrying a citizen of another country and acquiring the additional citizenship as a 'side effect' of the marriage, need not forfeit their Australian nationality as a result *if the law of the other country allows the person to retain their previous citizenship.* But if the Australian citizen marries a citizen of another country then applies to assume that foreign citizenship by registration or some other way, he/she may cease to be an Australian citizen.

Renunciation of citizenship

A person older than 18 may also renounce their Australian citizenship by completing a special form and by sending it to the Department of Immigration and Ethnic Affairs in Australia, or to the nearest Australian embassy or high commission, if they are outside the country. However, the government may refuse to approve the renunciation if the person would become stateless as a result (by having no other citizenship) or if the Minister for Immigration and Ethnic Affairs considers it is not in Australia's interest to grant the application.

Deprivation of citizenship

People may be deprived of their citizenship, inside or outside Australia, if:

- convicted of having provided false or misleading information, or concealing important information in applying for citizenship
- convicted in Australia or abroad of an offence committed before citizenship was granted and sentenced to death or imprisonment for twelve months or more
- their parent or guardian loses Australian citizenship, so

children under 18 may be deprived of Australian citizenship, too. However, the child(ren) would not be affected if this withdrawal would leave them stateless or if they have one responsible parent or guardian who remains an Australian citizen.

Resumption of citizenship

A person who loses Australian citizenship for any reason before his/her 18th birthday must make a declaration within a year of turning 18 that they wish to resume that citizenship. When Australia revised its citizenship laws in 1984 — changes fully effective from November 1986 — the Federal Government approved the repeal of **British Subject Status**. In the past, this had given the citizens of other member countries of the British Commonwealth some advantages in Australia. However, this repeal of old laws will *not* be effective around Australia until the State Governments update their legislation with regard to British subjects. As far as citizenship is concerned, immigrants from other Commonwealth countries must meet the same requirements for Australian citizenship as permanent residents from other countries.

The applicant must also

- intend to live in Australia permanently and
- maintain 'a close and continuing association with Australia'

according to the rules of the matter. But some people need not have lived in Australia for two years, as defined above. Provided the applicant is a permanent resident, the two-year rule may be waived if the person:

- is the husband, wife or widow of an Australian citizen
- is a child under the age of 16 included in a parent's application or
  if there are 'special circumstances' applying to children under 18 years of age
- has spent at least three months in Australia's permanent defence forces
- is a former Australian citizen or born in Australia. Such applicant can ask for citizenship again if they have lived in Australia as a permanent resident for 12 months in the previous two years.

People who have renounced Australian citizenship must wait at least 12 months before they can apply to become citizens again.

Applications abroad

It is usual for applicants to be living in Australia when they apply for citizenship and to be available for interview to determine good character and for the citizenship ceremony which follows; but citizenship can be granted under certain circumstances to people living abroad. In such unusual cases, Australian citizenship can be granted in another country to:

- spouses, widows or widowers of Australian citizens
- children adopted overseas by Australian citizens
- persons engaged in activities overseas which the Minister for Immigration and Ethnic Affairs considers beneficial to the interests of Australia

Such people must have been approved for permanent residence and plan to live in Australia and 'maintain a close and continuing association' with Australia.

Other citizenship requirements

The other requirements for people hoping to be approved for Australian citizenship include the ability to speak and understand basic English; to understand the responsibilities and privileges of Australian citizenship, and to be of good character. However, some people are exempt from requirements regarding knowledge of English and privileges of Australian citizenship if they are spouses, widows or widowers of Australian citizens, suffer a substantial hearing, speech or sight disability, or are older than 60.

Children born in Australia or one of its territories have an automatic right to citizenship. Children born outside Australia to Australian parent(s) can be registered as citizens under the law of citizenship by descent. The parent(s), or guardian(s) if the Australian parent(s) are dead or no longer have legal custody of the child, can apply on behalf of the child. If the child is 18 or more, it is *not possible* for them to acquire Australian citizenship this way.

People who have gained citizenship by descent *cannot* register their children as citizens unless the parent(s) has been legally present in Australia for at least two years at any time before the date of application for registration. However, people who become Australian citizens by other means than by descent — those who were born there — can apply to have their children under the age of 18 registered as Australian citizens by descent, whether or not they or the children have lived there.

6
Foreign Qualifications and Studying in Australia

This chapter has two aims. It is a guide for prospective:

- **private overseas students**

  Are you wanting to come to Australia temporarily, as a student? Australia has comprehensive facilities for this, and actively encourages students of certain origins to take advantage of the multitude of tertiary and training facilities it offers at the Government's universities and colleges.

- **professionals and skilled migrants**

  Do you have qualifications, degrees, certificates or other proof of a skill, expertise or education gained which you need to practice your trade or profession in Australia? There is a special Australian education body, the Commission on Overseas Professional Qualifications (COPQ) available to assist you. However school and university age students, and their parents should see the Chapter on **Australian Education.**

COMMISSION ON OVERSEAS PROFESSIONAL QUALIFICATIONS (COPQ)

Are you hoping to *migrate* under the Employer Nomination or Skills in Demand categories, or to open a business or provide a service which entails you practising a trade or profession? Whatever the grounds for your migration, application to COPQ will probably be necessary. Migration authorities will advise you on whether you definitely need COPQ's recognition of your training or expertise to work in your field.

Even if you are only going to Australia for a *temporary posting* with an employer, or as a *working holidaymaker*, you may need COPQ's recognition in order to work in your trade or profession. Once again, authorities at the Australian embassy or high commission where the application is made will tell you if you need to check with COPQ.

Alternatively, if your trip there does *not* depend on your employability in that skill or profession, and if you are permitted to work by your visa (if a non-resident), assessment can be made by COPQ when you are already in Australia.

Since the late 1960s, COPQ has set up and expanded **panels** and **advisory councils** to check that foreign educational and training qualifications parallel the standards and knowledge expected of people practising in a particular field in Australia.

Often, a degree or certificate from a recognised educational institution in an English-speaking country will present few complications for assessment. If you have *not* received an English-language education, or speak it as a first or mother tongue, COPQ will arrange for you to be examined for your ability to speak, read and write English to a standard acceptable to that profession in Australia.

Heavy demand

However, funding restrictions on COPQ in recent years means the scope and speed of assessment may be limited. Some 10,000 people a year apply to its panels and councils. There has been a major increase in demand on its facilities to assess foreigners hoping to practice in fields like nursing, engineering, computing, occupational therapy, or with teaching and technical as well as general academic qualifications. In some cases, by the time you have a qualification assessed and/or arrange for oral or written examinations — whether within Australia or waiting for permission to go there — many months may have elapsed.

Assessment methods

COPQ panels rely on examinations or some other form of assessment relevant to the skill or profession an applicant hopes to practise in Australia. COPQ has evolved a system of formal examinations and assessments designed by experts in Australia to help assess the qualifications of people hoping to work in Australia in the following fields:

- dentistry
- medicine
- nursing
- dietetics
- pharmacy
- physiotherapy
- occupational therapy
- veterinary science
- occupational English

(An examination in podiatry was being introduced, at the time of writing.) However, the failure rate is often high. COPQ is lobbying the Federal Government for more money to fund a programme of **reorienting bridging courses**. It hopes to develop this for people with different training backgrounds to those commonly encountered by and acceptable to their would-be Australian colleagues.

Fees
Whether the applicant passes or fails, fees are charged for certain examinations as well as for some COPQ literature. The table gives a guide to amounts you can expect to pay in 1987 in Australian dollars or equivalent in another currency, but note that these may change as time goes on.

Scale of Fees	
For Occupational English examination	$A60
For Occupational Therapy examination	$A100
For Dietetics examination	$A100
For Veterinary Science examination (two papers)	$A300 x 2
For General Academic Qualifications certificates	$A20
For publication, *World Summary*	$A10
For publication, *The Compendium of Overseas Qualifications*	$A50
For publication, *Assessing Authorities in Australia*	$A10

Assessment policy
There is a certain amount of politics and power-play in these assessments. Australians who are already in professional, technical and other jobs requiring high levels of education or training are naturally keen to protect their market and earning-power against competition from newcomers. Furthermore, foreign training often has aspects to it not covered in Australia, and vice versa. Yet Australian governments, and those with the best interests of the community in mind, realise that rejection of many applicants could mean missing out on an international pool of talent and expertise essential to building up industry and society.

Additionally, people with a non-English language background may find that Australian professionals regard foreign qualifications with some reservations. Many migrants are forced to work in less-than-adequate jobs, considering the standard of their education, if not recognised by their Australian colleagues via COPQ assessment.

AUSTRALIAN PROFESSIONS AND COPQ

Generally, the national ruling bodies of the various professions require an immigrant to have qualifications recognised by them, before he or she can legally work in that profession in Australia. In this respect, the professional associations in Australia are rather like trade unions operating a 'closed shop' policy. Professional organisations and associations represent the interests of their members to the public as well as governments in Australia. They actively lobby and advise on fees, working conditions and enforce a code of conduct for their members.

COPQ relies on the services and advice of hundreds of Australian professional experts through its system of panels and advisory councils. Would-be entrants to professions in Australia, needing approval to practice, should contact these organisations directly or via COPQ or Australian embassies and high commissions for specific information about the particular profession.

COPQ has expert panels drawn from Australian professional organisations in the following fields:

- accountancy
- architecture
- computing
- dietetics
- general academic qualifications
- occupational english
- occupational therapy
- podiatry
- social welfare
- technical qualifications
- teaching
- veterinary science

There are two sub-committees to assess dental technicians and draftsmen. As mentioned earlier in this Chapter, there are examination procedures already established for foreign applicants in the professions of occupational English, occupational therapy, dietetics and veterinary science, with podiatry also planned. Other professions require practitioners who want to practice in Australia to pass standard Australian examinations.

Further information
Commission on Overseas Professional Qualifications, Commerce House, Cnr Brisbane Avenue and Macquarie Street, Barton, ACT 2600, Australia. Tel: 062-705711.

OVERSEAS STUDENTS

More than 10,000 foreign students study at Australian universities and tertiary colleges each year. A limited number of places are set aside annually for people from abroad to start full-time courses at high schools, tertiary colleges and universities. All applicants are welcome, but must meet certain academic, language and social requirements *and* pay the fees. Since the number of places available is tight, and held at the same level in recent years, competition for temporary entry is strong. In 1987, the quota for new foreign students starting courses at Australian secondary colleges and high schools was set at 1,500 — and another 2,000 were allowed to start their studies at universities and colleges of technical or further education.

Australia's Federal Government considers the following educational and foreign policy factors to be particularly important in accepting overseas students:

- the capacity of Australian academic institutions to accept overseas students without displacing Australian students
- Australia's interest in the countries of origin
- the degree of support or sponsorship by the applicants' home government
- the relative academic standards of the applying students and their standard of competence in English
- the content and duration of their proposed course and the value to the applicants' home countries
- the opportunities for equivalent studies in the home country or country of residence in each case, so as not to disadvantage local students

Financial cutbacks in education in recent years have also contributed to a less benevolent approach to allowing foreign students to use Australia's facilities in order to foster international goodwill or as part of its aid programmes. Nevertheless, scholarship and fellowship (sponsored) students continue to come at the expense of Australia's or their own governments, or — more commonly — because they have gained a place as private students.

Sponsored students
Sponsored students are nominated by their own governments to take part

in Australia's technical co-operation schemes under its overseas aid programme. Usually this involves young people from Third World countries. Training assistance is provided on a government-to-government basis, with Australia aiming to help the economic and social advancement of each student's home country.

Other governments involved in the student sponsorship programme — usually in the South Pacific and South-East Asian regions — relate their training and educational requests of Australia, to priority areas for national development. **Nominations** are accepted from agencies or authorities approved by nominating governments; they are made through Australian diplomatic offices in the country of origin. An award of a place at an Australian university or college is made only after the candidate has been formally accepted by the appropriate university or college administration. Mostly, such awards of scholarships or fellowships are at **postgraduate** level. They cover the cost of travel to and from Australia and living allowances while the student is there.

Private overseas students

Australia's programme of education for private overseas students is administered by the **Overseas Students' Office** (OSO) within the Federal Department of Education. The programme is competitive and expensive; the policy is to charge for half the cost of tuition — while students must also be able to support themselves and their dependants in Australia. They must be studying full-time courses but are allowed to take part-time jobs (up to 20 hours a week — see below) only.

Applications must be lodged at an Australian embassy or high commission in the applicant's country of citizenship if they wish to take up:

- formal studies — tertiary studies at technical and further education (TAFE) college level or tertiary studies at undergraduate or postgraduate level
- an English language course
- occupational (on-the-job) or religious training
- special studies at a private, fee-paying institution (for example secretarial and business colleges, or pilot training)
- study of miscellaneous subjects at a university or college of advanced education or other publicly-funded institution which does *not* lead to an award of a degree or similar qualification
- studies under exchange arrangements such as Rotary Youth Exchange between Australian and overseas educational institutions.

If you are thinking of applying as a private overseas student, or for a scholarship to study under a fellowship or similar award, you must make it quite clear to Australia's authorities at the embassy or high commission in your country of citizenship that you:

1. genuinely seek temporary entry to Australia for **study purposes** only
2. wish to enrol in an **approved course** of study at a university or college
3. have adequate **competence in English** for the course you propose to study (see further details on language competence below)
4. have a **financial guarantor** able and willing to cover all your expenses during the stay in Australia, including return air fares and tuition fees (see **Fees** later in this section)
5. are of **good health and character**

Students can obtain information about courses and educational institutions in Australia from the embassy or high commission; they should do so before lodging a formal application to various universities and colleges in Australia, via an embassy or high commmission. Bear in mind that the Australian academic year may be quite different from that of your own country. It runs from February to December, and tertiary institutions usually have semesters with short breaks between and a summer holiday lasting about two months, following examinations in December.

FEES

Candidates must pay an application fee ($A50 at the time of writing) on lodgement of the application. Tuition fees in Australia, which have been extended to cover most courses for private (non-sponsored) overseas students, are meant to cover half the cost of the course at publicly-funded institutions. These fees are increased regularly, to account for inflation. As a guide, overseas students at secondary schools were required to pay $A300 a year in 1986-87. Students at colleges of technical and further education (TAFE) were required to pay $A740 a year in 1987.

Fees at universities and colleges of further education are far greater than that; for example, private students from overseas admitted to study medicine, dentistry and veterinary science in 1987 were charged fees of $A5,506 a year, and $A3,056 a year for other courses.

If admitted to a *non*-government school or college, the fees could be very much higher even than these.

ADDITIONAL COSTS OF LIVING AND STUDYING IN AUSTRALIA

Additional costs like books, union fees at tertiary institutions, and school uniforms (at high schools) must also be considered in planning your budget for living in Australia as a private overseas student. From 1987, *all* tertiary students in Australia — except in cases of financial hardship —must pay an administrative charge of $A250.

The cost of living in Australia for a student not at a boarding school, was at least $A12,000 a year by the late 1980s. Residential areas in big university cities like Sydney and Melbourne close to universities have become 'gentrified' in recent years; rents are quite high if the student does not have a place at a campus college. If married, the student should budget another $A5,000 a year for a spouse and at least $A2,500 a year for each child. These estimates do *not* include airfares and student fees.

As mentioned in the Chapter on **Australian Health and Welfare**, anyone with permission to stay in Australia longer than six months generally qualifies for Medicare and only nominal charges are made for visits to doctors, medicines and hospital treatment. Extras, as may be necessary for a young family or if you or your dependants have chronic illnesses, may be bought from private health funds.

ENGLISH LANGUAGE REQUIREMENTS

All applicants must have a knowledge of written and spoken English adequate for the level of the courses they propose to study. If English is not their mother tongue or the language in which they have gained their previous educational qualifications, applicants must pass the **Short Selection Test** (SST) — the official test of English language proficiency for entry to Australian courses. The test is supervised by the Australian embassy or high commission in the country where students have lodged their applications; there is a charge ($A35 at time of writing). A sample test kit is available ($A15, at time of writing), so students can gauge their capacity to pass the test and show the Australian authorities they can understand and express themselves in English adequately for study purposes.

However, the SST will not be necessary if you are:

- a student whose first language is English
- a student applying for undergraduate or postgraduate studies who has successfully completed secondary or undergraduate courses in an English-speaking country

- a student who has scored 550 or more on the American Test of English as a Foreign Language (TOEFL). Students undertaking the TOEFL should have their scores sent directly to the Overseas Students' Office (OSO) by marking the institution code, 9193, on their test admission ticket and answer sheet, otherwise the original score report must be sent with the application form to the OSO
- someone who has taken the SST since January 1985 and passed, in which case you must send a copy of the certificate
- a Hong Kong educated applicant who has obtained a pass at C grade or better in English in the GCE O-Level examinations
- a Fijian or Tongan applicant for undergraduate entry who has obtained a score of 50 per cent or more in English in the New Zealand university entrance examination. Applicants for senior secondary/matriculation entry must have obtained a score of 60 per cent or more in English in the New Zealand School Certificate
- an applicant who has passed the selection test for schools via the Freeman Overseas Testing Service (FOTS). However, schools satisfied by FOTS are only some of the many Australian schools which welcome overseas students at secondary level.

STUDY AT JUNIOR SECONDARY LEVEL

Only nationals of certain countries can apply for entry to Australian schools at junior secondary level. These countries are Papua New Guinea and ten sovereign states of the South Pacific (the Solomon Islands, Vanuatu, Nauru, Fiji, Tonga, Kiribati, Tuvalu, Western Samoa, Cook Islands and Niue). Generally, students (from the age of about 13 to 16, at junior secondary level) are expected to live in boarding schools, which are usually run privately and have high fees.

STUDY AT SENIOR SECONDARY LEVEL

Senior secondary students of any nationality are welcome to attend private or government schools if they meet English language, financial, educational, health and character criteria already mentioned. In addition, they must pay 45 per cent of the cost of their tuition at government secondary schools, or the even higher fees charged by private (non-government) schools, often many thousands of dollars a year.

Unlike students applying for tertiary education in Australia, secondary school applicants must *not* make arrangements with educational institutions in Australia directly, other than confirming a place would be available for them.

Applications should be made to the local Australian embassy or high commission which will, in turn, contact State Departments of Education. Applicants may nominate the non-government school of their choice and up to three Australian States or Territories where they would like to attend a TAFE matriculation course or high school. Students should also indicate whether they want to complete their senior secondary education at a matriculation course run by a TAFE in preference to an Australian high school. Applicants for non-government schools must first obtain offers of a place, and include a letter from the school making this offer among other documentation in the application.

FINANCIAL GUARANTEES

When making their applications, private overseas students are required to sign a declaration stating they are aware of the likely costs of study in Australia and that someone, either the student, a parent or guardian, has the capacity to meet these costs. Private students who cannot pay the Overseas Students' Charge, or support themselves there, will have their stay in Australia terminated and be required to return to their home country.

WORK AND TAXES

A private overseas student is permitted to take a part-time job on a 'casual' basis (as non-permanent staff and therefore having no right to holiday pay or other 'permanent' conditions) for up to 20 hours a week. However, he/she will be allowed to work full-time during vacations. But if the student fails the course and blames the job, Australian authorities will not accept this excuse as reason for extending the stay in the country. As for tax, a student who stays more than six months must complete a **taxation rebate declaration** form and be treated as a resident of Australia in terms of obligation to pay taxes. He/she will be allowed the usual tax-free amount before the regular Australian income taxes become chargeable (see Chapter 9).

DEPENDANTS

As a rule, foreign students awarded a place at an Australian institution within their country's quota must go to Australia alone and apply for spouses or children to join them later. However, it is feasible for students to apply in advance to the Australian embassy or high commission to leave with their spouses and children. *The student's visa application must include this request.*

Dependants of student applicants may themselves undertake courses of education in Australia without being counted in their country's quota. However, they will have to pay the Overseas Students' Charge for formal courses leading to an award of a diploma or degree from a university, college or other institution where they hope to study.

The spouse of an overseas student is allowed to work in Australia, though the authorities warn that this may be easier said than done — bearing in mind the delays and complications in gaining recognition of professional qualifications, if any, and high unemployment generally. However, overseas students hoping to take a spouse or children with them must prove to the Australian authorities they can cover each dependant's living expenses anyway.

In the case of sponsored (scholarship) students, the Australian government does *not* pay for dependants' travel expenses; however in some cases maintenance will be paid to the family in Australia. All dependants must leave Australia when the overseas students finishes his/her course.

ACCOMMODATION

Overseas students and their families must arrange their own housing in Australia, though they may be met on arrival and given some help finding accommodation. The **Coordinating Committee for Overseas Students** operates in all States and Territories of Australia (except Tasmania and the Australian Capital Territory). It is equipped to help with housing; students who think they might need this service should write to the Committee in the appropriate State or Territory as soon as possible before leaving for Australia.

Further information
Australian Department of Education,
Overseas Students' Office,
PO Box 25,
Woden, ACT 2606,
Australia.
The addresses of the Coordinating Committees for the OSO may be obtained through the OSO in Australia, or from the Australian embassy or high commission where enquiries are made.

7
Business Migration — Locations and Incentives

BUSINESS MIGRATION INCENTIVES

Each State and Territory of Australia wants new people who can bring commercial know-how and capital with them. Conversely, would-be settlers in every migration category — business or otherwise — are wise to assess each of Australia's six States and two Territories. Apart from friends, family or other reasons that may predispose you to settle in a particular area, considering the lifestyle of a location will help you make the most of Australia.

Choice of location

An ill-advised choice of location in Australia will add to the traumas of newcomers trying to fit in. There is a certain sameness about the buildings, food, climate and casual style of the most heavily populated coastal towns and cities where most people live and work. But the atmospheric and cultural emphases vary from State to State, and from coast to coast.

Apart from the advice of friends, relatives, or governments at various levels about whether and where settlers from your own country would be happy and tend to congregate, it is vital to examine the relevant trade, commerce, industry and job opportunities in places you consider living. Each State and Territory authority has a range of **business incentives** for ventures of all sizes. These may include:

- tax rebates
- free counselling and computer services
- loan guarantees and even cash grants for business

Some State Governments will virtually guide you through the paperwork and red tape, particularly if you are deemed a desirable business migrant, issuing checklists of the precise information needed for a successful application.

Some Australian States will also be able to advise newcomers where to invest their money, if they have no specific venture ideas of their own. They may produce regularly updated lists of 'business opportunities'. Bear in mind, however, that these proposed 'opportunities' will *not* be enough to win a would-be migrant approval for permanent residence in Australia — though of course the intention to enter into a new or expanding venture encouraged by regional authorities is a great help to your case.

Immigration officials can put you in touch with Australian **trade commissioners** for counselling and personal contacts helpful for your plans. State government offices are maintained around the world, and their literature and representatives are also available via Australian embassies and high commissions. The States are extremely competitive in their desire to attract foreign investors and business migrants. All the States and Territories pride themselves on being 'flexible', with the ability to look at each potential venture, no matter how modest, and advise individuals on where and whether they would have the best chance of success. A would-be immigrant may also be told if another part of the country is likely to be more attracted to his or her specific talents, expertise or product. The State Governments can and do apply for migration permission from the Federal Government authorities, if they need to be convinced — as they sometimes do — that a particular applicant has a business proposition which is viable.

Commercial information

Through Australia's State or Territory governments, you can be referred to relevant commercial organisations for the latest information on the types of business you are contemplating. Local chambers of commerce (representing businesspeople in an area), professional associations or state-run small business advisory services are there to help with information about cost of living, disposable income, employment rates, business earnings and so forth which, as 'moving targets', cannot be accurately detailed in this book. Their help is usually free of charge. However, some vital statistics for each state and territory are listed over the page.

Here is a resumé of each State and Territory, and government incentives for business people.

SOUTH AUSTRALIA

South Australia promotes itself as the ideal combination of leisure and culture. You may well agree, especially if you establish yourself in or

Exports by State — Australian Produce
(Manufactured or Otherwise)
Annual Value in Australian Dollars
From July 1985 to June 1986
(*Source*: Australian Bureau of Statistics)

	$A
New South Wales (NSW)	7,373,750,000
Victoria (Vict)	6,806,068,000
Queensland (Qld)	7,606,400,000
South Australia (South Aust)	1,988,233,000
Western Australia (West Aust)	6,516,203,000
Tasmania	900,011,000
Northern Territory (NT)	603,747,000
Australian Capital Territory (ACT — Canberra)	3,834,000
(Australian produce *not* attributable to state of origin	121,212,000

Average Weekly Total Earnings
(Male and Female Average) in Australian Dollars
(*Source*: Australian Bureau of Statistics, August 1986)

NSW	Vict	Qld	South Aust	West Aust	Tas	NT	ACT
454.10	439.50	425.10	426.00	448.50	428.40	490.20	490.90

Total Unemployed Persons (Male and Female),
as a percentage of the
Australian full-time workforce, of about 3.9 million people
(*Source*: Australian Bureau of Statistics, December 1986)

NSW	Vict	Qld	South Aust	West Aust	Tas	NT	ACT
8.6	7.3	10.2	9.1	8.1	10.0	6.0	5.4

near Adelaide, its capital city of just under a million people. Certainly, living and working in suburban South Australia is a fine compromise for many migrants. Adelaide offers much of the beauty and sophistication of Australia's bigger capitals (Sydney, Melbourne, Brisbane) without their wretched excesses, such as high land prices and traffic jams.

Adelaide has a thriving cultural life and a biannual Arts Festival attracting the cream of Australian talent and innovation. Yet it has a relatively conservative aura, since South Australia was always a 'free' colony, not a convict centre. Tourist literature used to bill Adelaide as Australia's city of churches, reflecting the state's 'wholesome' history as a free Christian society.

But this is not considered a marketable or accurate image of Adelaide in the late twentieth century. So current promotional campaigns skip the churches — hyping the capital with slogans like 'Adelaide Alive' and promising 'the country's most opulent and ornate casino'.

The State Government is also keen to remind Australians and everyone else that Adelaide is host to annual Grand Prix Formula One competitions Down Under until 1992, and has been voted the world's best venue by the international racing jet-set.

Adelaide has plenty of stylish pubs, bars and restaurants. A flashy nightlife reflects the fact it is a minor gay capital. A succession of progressive governments — both Labor and Liberal — have set examples for other States and Territories with civil, social and sexual reforms since the 1970s.

South Australian towns and properties boast graceful buildings of predominantly English and German style. Its people are proud of their history and heritage of free settlement. The famous bluestone homes and public buildings of Adelaide are among the most orderly and best cared for examples of colonial architecture in the country.

Leisure
Holiday attractions for locals and tourist resorts are varied: from the mysterious 'blue lake' of Mount Gambier, extensive bird and wildlife reserves, magnificent rocky coast, to some of the best restaurants in the country, many in lovely winegrowing settings. There is also plenty of orange and ochre desert, including the driest area in Australia, rugged mountain ranges and fabulous national parks, as well as many unspoilt beaches near its main urban centres.

Trade
South Australia has 1.34 million people and 16 million sheep. It is a hub of activity for Australia's export of farm goods and is the nation's biggest producer of wine and barley. Would-be immigrants planning to

start export-oriented projects will soon see that it is, as State Government advisers point out, a 'cost-effective' location for sea transport of primary produce to Australian or foreign customers. This is already big business, for South Australia is a major exporter of live sheep and beef abroad. It is ideally placed for domestic trade routes, halfway between Australia's main coastal population centres to the east and the west.

International shipping facilities at Whyalla, Port Augusta, Port Pirie and Port Lincoln are well-located for serving established markets in the Pacific Basin region as well as the Middle East, the USA and Europe while Portland, a major deep sea port, is just 100 km over the border in Victoria.

South Australia boasts the best industrial relations in the nation (ie — the least strikes of any state) while wages are estimated to be around 10 per cent lower than in other places. It has the world's largest uranium and copper mine at Roxby Downs and the biggest lead smelting plant, as well as substantial reserves of oil and gas — all encouraging for development of manufacturing and high technology ventures.

Historically, the state is base for heavy industries in Australia, such as car building and whitegoods manufacturing. Again, it is well sited and set up for exports and imports. The Government and private sector are co-operating in an effort to market its products more professionally and aggressively.

State policy

The State Labor Government has a coherent approach to encouraging enterprises of all sizes to locate themselves within its borders and, like some of its 'competitor' states, publishes lists of 'business opportunities' for would-be immigrants unsure of how they want to invest money and energy in Australia. The next page contains a sample showing the range of ventures for which South Australians have sought immigrant investment in the past.

As well as specific business opportunities 'advertised' through the State Government to prospective investors and immigrants, South Australia has other programmes providing incentives for what the Government likes to call 'the big thinkers' from outside. Its industrial incentives programme, for which certain projects qualify, features

- cash payments for establishing businesses
- guarantees of commercial loans
- payroll tax rebates for regional locations

The payroll tax rebates and land tax reimbursements for approved manufacturing and processing industries exemplify South Australia's

Recent Business Opportunities

Established mechanical engineering company seeking an equity partner to further develop production capacity. The company manufactures engine components for motor vehicles and a variety of precision instruments for all mechanical operations. Investment: $A150,000 plus.

Sportswear manufacturer (domestic market). Turnover $A1 million per annum, gross profit $A398,000. Twenty employees plus subcontractors. 25% to 75% equity available. Sale of business of $A500,000 (including real estate $A95,000 and machinery $A65,000). Relatively young business with good market recognition and potential for expansion.

A small boutique winery in the Barossa Valley 40 km from Adelaide is for sale. The company's wines are marketed throughout Australia and to markets in the USA, Canada and New Guinea. Sales turnover about $A800,000. It is noted the company has a loan of 1.2 million Swiss francs maturing May 1989. Ideally, the purchaser should have a strong background in marketing and an interest in developing export opportunities. Owners are seeking $A2 million for the winery and associated facilities.

willingness to forego revenue as a form of long-term investment in the economy.

Though prime office rents are nearly 40 per cent cheaper in Adelaide than in Melbourne and around 65 per cent less than in Sydney, South Australians are keen to move their population, consumption and industrial centres from Adelaide and the nearby port cities into more sparsely populated places. Yet, even in desirable countryside locations an hour's drive from Adelaide proper, like the Barossa Valley winegrowing and south coast districts, State tax reimbursements and rebates on land and payroll taxes apply. Each proposal made to the local authorities in the hope of qualifying for various concessions is assessed on individual merits. The authorities are prepared to tailor their offers and incentives to specific needs of applicants, in the drive to develop South Australia's economy and markets.

Most of South Australia's manufacturing effort is based in and around Adelaide, though the Spencer Gulf cities, the Green Triangle, and Riverland Regions are also involved. The factory construction scheme offers all sorts of incentives to approved projects, like

- 100 per cent finance to cover land and building costs
- low interest rates on mortgages
- rents for factory premises fixed at leases applying for 11 years

The Department of State Development of South Australia maintains a **register of industrial land and premises** available from both the private and public sectors for lease and sale in the Adelaide area. Details of zoning, location, land size, buildings size, general description and real estate agents for these properties are included in the service. **Site studies** assess suitable industrial locations for projects in South Australia — in terms of access to raw materials and energy, markets, infrastructure, services and transport.

There are other financial arrangements available through the Government, to encourage those who could offer new jobs and investment by starting a commercial venture or expanding an old one.

Small businesses in South Australia
At the other end of the scale, the State has facilities to help small ventures get off the ground. Many applicants approved as business migrants go to South Australia to start modest consultancy services of various types. Often they are based on relatively small amounts of finance but impressive personal expertise. The **Small Business Corporation** is an independent authority, founded by Act of Parliament to provide information, counselling and grants of up to half the cost of consultancy work. It can be a useful contact and, through it, State Government loan guarantees, a Computer Advisory Centre, data processing and other services are available.

Further Information
Director of Development, Department of State Development, GPO Box 1264, Adelaide, 5001. Telephone (Australia) (08) 210 8333. South Australia also has representatives in London, Los Angeles, Tokyo, Singapore, and Hong Kong. Or contact the nearest Australian High Commission, Embassy or Trade Commission.

QUEENSLAND

Queensland is one of the most wonderful holiday locations in the world — so it follows that actually working for a living there should be nice, too. Thousands of Australians buy holiday homes and eventually move to Queensland's popular coastal resorts when they retire, in order to enjoy the vivid tropical environment where they can swim in the blue Pacific all year round.

Rugged conservatism
Queensland typifies the luxurious, laid-back'n'leisurely Aussie lifestyle, but its interior is largely dry, rugged and backward, rather than laid-

back. The State is a conservative bastion, run by Sir Joh Bjelke-Petersen's ultra-right wing National party for two decades. Queenslanders — also known as 'banana benders' — often build their houses on stilts and decorate their vast wooden verandahs with distinctive coloured glass. They drink beer in pots (10oz glasses) not schooners (14oz glasses) because, they argue, the stuff warms up so fast in the heat. Queenslanders are also said to talk slower than other Aussies, and with a more pronounced drawl than to the south.

The poor condition of Aboriginals on the reserves of the far north, allegations of political 'gerrymandering' to keep Sir Joh's National Party in power, strong-arm tactics against striking unions and conservationists...not to mention controversial laws allowing a publican to refuse to serve homosexuals and 'sexual deviants', are among the issues that still make Queenslanders something of a laughing stock among Australia's southern 'sophisticates'. In many senses Queensland certainly lives up to its reputation as the 'deep north' — Australia's answer to the southern states of the USA. In retaliation, the occupants of the Sunshine State sometimes refer to their fellow Australians from south of the border as 'Mexicans'...and drawl that critics of Queensland are just jealous.

Queensland's economic life

The Queensland Government is Australia's most active when it comes to accepting foreign investment and ownership in the name of economic progress, but average weekly income is lower and unemployment higher than in any other State or Territory (see the statistics at the front of this Chapter). The Premier, Sir Joh (who nominated himself for a knighthood), has been accused of putting the business of exploiting Queenland's vast mineral and agricultural resources ahead of more humane considerations.

However, the fact is that Queensland earns more export income than any other Australian State. Both foreign and domestic investors find the Government's policies most comforting. Goodness gracious — as Sir Joh would say — the State Government must be doing something right: even its arch enemies, those 'socialists' running the Canberra Labor Government, have dramatically reduced restrictions on foreigners buying into real estate, primary industry, tourism and manufacturing, echoing Queensland's way of encouraging growth.

The possibilities for money to be made from wealthy resident and tourist consumers, a big country, and the attitude of its Government to investment, attract both active entrepreneurs and semi-retired settlers from abroad. **Tourism** presents a wealth of business opportunities, both for foreign investors and people who live there. The Great Barrier Reef is a wonder of the natural world and the so-called Gold and Sunshine

Coasts of the south-east, where hotels, casinos, and apartments now cast afternoon shadows along miles of beaches, are the State's main tourist attractions. Tropical islands are fast being developed as tourist resorts, while visits to the outback and tropical jungles north of Cairns are also great attractions for Australians and foreigners alike, wanting a rich, novel experience.

Queensland is a leading exporter of Australian raw foodstuffs and minerals. Coal is the biggest export commodity though copper, crude lead, bauxite as well as tropical fruits and other agricultural products pour out of the State's 19 ports for consumption and processing in Australia and elsewhere. The Government is keen to develop the State's huge oil deposits and expand mining projects extracting and reprocessing bauxite, tin, lead, zinc, silver and gold. International price pressures in the past decade have led to rationalisation by some of Queensland's agricultural and mineral exporters — particularly sugar cane products — due to the world price drop in sugar.

However, multinationals and millionaires are not the sole targets of the Queensland Government's policy of encouraging business to get on with it. The State Government offers a range of aid programmes for commercial ventures of all sizes through the **Queensland Industry Development Corporation**. The State holds reserves of fully serviced industrial land which can be obtained on 30-year leases with discounted rental rates over the first five years. There are also financial guarantees to help businesses raise capital. Grants and loans upwards of $A20,000 are also offered to approved businesses. All sorts of finance — from hire purchase, lease finance and short or long-term export finance are available through the QIDC.

As a relatively new body, the QIDC proposes a prime lending rate as a reference point for all negotiated loans. The cost of loans is geared to the applicant's capacity to repay and interest rates will either be on a fixed rate of interest or on a fluctuating-rate basis.

Queensland, like the other States, is keen to move from primary and mining exports into **high technology** industries and has two technology parks — one at Labrador, on the Gold Coast, and another at Eight Mile Plains, a south-west suburb of the state capital, Brisbane.

Business incentives also include

- construction of factory buildings under special circumstances on Crown industrial estates for ventures the government is persuaded would be of long-term benefit
- State finance-raising assistance for approved ventures
- relocation subsidies for upgrading businesses

Government aid is also offered for companies wanting to develop

export markets through a loan scheme for payment of necessary air fares for business and promotion trips. Queensland also has an advisory service for **small business** administered by its Department of Industrial Development. Queensland further encourages domestic and international trade by offering subsidies to cover up to half the cost of moving new export products either within Australia or outside the country. This subsidy applies to general manufacturing industries (not food processing or minerals) and extends to the inward carriage of certain raw materials (excluding all forms of fabricated steel).

Food processing industries can claim a subsidy on inward carriage and packaging materials if these are not available locally. The incentive aims at decentralising Queenland's manufacturing sector by compensating companies for the greater distances they must cover to transport materials and finished goods.

Like some of Australia's other States, Queensland keeps a **register of business opportunities** which would-be immigrants might like to consider, if at a loss for a project that would make them attractive to that State. The examples shown in the box, though no longer current, indicate

---

Recent Business Opportunities in Queensland

Solar-powered boat — a unique invention which uses no fuel at all to propel itself, but relies on solar energy to compress air through a manifold storage tank. A small valve allows the driver to control the airflow into the motor and therefore the speed of the propeller. A prototype has already been built and tested. Funds are needed to continue with detailed tests and analyses by Queensland University before starting to produce solar-powered boats for sale in Australia and overseas. Project needs direct investment or joint venture agreement providing capital of at least $A50,000.

Mount Magnus/Darling Downs Fruit Juices — fruit juice business, apple orchard, winery and tourist property for sale. Situated on 40 hectares (100 acres) about 200 km from Brisbane. Improvements include 3,300 square metres of buildings, public tasting cellars, 2,300 metres of cold storage, three brick homes and workers' quarters. Price: $A500,000 negotiable.

Farm tourism — for investment. Cunningham's Cape area about one and a half hours' drive from Brisbane. The property has a one-mile highway frontage and a total area of 474 acres, of which 133 are being cultivated for grain. The property has four tourist cabins and the shire council has approved development of a caravan park. Investment sought: $A375,000.

the kinds of ventures encouraged by the Queensland Government in recent years.

Further Information
Queensland Industry Development Corporation, GPO Box 1415, Brisbane, 4001, Queensland. Also Commercial and Industrial Development Department, 160 Anne Street, Brisbane 4000, Queensland. The Queensland Government has representatives in London, Tokyo and Bahrain. Or contact the nearest Australian High Commission, Embassy or Trade Commission.

VICTORIA

Victoria is a state with an old-fashioned flavour, both in its physical manifestations and quality of life. There is an on-going battle between the State capital, Australia's second biggest city, Melbourne, and that even more populated sprawl over the border in New South Wales, Sydney. Melbourne to Sydney is like a gentlemen's club compared to a strip joint — or so they'll say in Victoria. In their newspapers and chat shows Sydney-siders sneer about the awful flatness of Melbourne's suburban wasteland compared to Sydney's leafy harbour-frontages. The Victorians snipe back about the high crime rate, stinking beaches and rip-offs in food and entertainment up north. Melbourne's superior restaurants, its intellectual, fashion and theatrical leadership, and scintillating dinner party conversation are regularly trotted out in the on-going competition with sexy, brash Sydney. Victoria's rolling rural countryside and well-preserved examples of British colonial architecture are the pride and joy of those who favour life in the smallest and second-oldest mainland State. People who love living in Australia generally are thrilled by the stunning mountains, bush landscape, secluded beaches and some of the best coastline to be seen anywhere.

Victoria's upper crust
The wealthy 'squatocracy' in and around Melbourne are traditionally political leaders of the nation, and Australia's most prestigious private boarding schools are located here. The members of Australia's 'upper crust' are to be found in the elegant drawing rooms and country estates of Victoria.

Multicultural Melbourne
Melbourne, home to 3 million people, is multicultural in flavour, with a thriving ethnic media, cultural, educational and restaurant scene. It boasts some of the best Italian food outside Italy and a China Town to

rival that of Sydney or even New York for quality, cheapness and variety of oriental cuisine. Melbourne's best-established sub-cultures are of Italian, Greek and Eastern European Jewish origins.

Financial centre
Melbourne remains a financial hub, despite the rise of gaudy *nouveaux riches*, wheeler-dealers and flashy stock exchange activity in Sydney and Perth. Some 70 per cent of capital committed to manufacturing and mining projects in Australia is authorised by companies based in Melbourne. Of the top ten multinational companies operating in Australia, seven are based in Melbourne and it is home for about half, by capitalisation, of the nation's 100 biggest companies. Victoria's finance and business sector employs over 500,000 people and accounts for 11 per cent of that State's Gross Domestic Product. Melbourne-based firms underwrite around three-quarters of all listed equity raisings and 88 per cent of all listed corporate fixed-interest debt raisings in Australia.

Manufacturing in Victoria
The Victorian Labor government calculates that its residents are the wealthiest per capita of any state in Australia. Though it has not the boom atmosphere of, say, Western Australia or Queensland, industrial and resource developments are significant — with three major projects starting up in the mid-1980s: an aluminium smelter joint venture in Portland, the huge Chia property development in Melbourne's chic South Yarra (the largest urban development ever undertaken in Australia), and Esso-BHP's oil and gas development programme in the Bass Strait.

About 30 per cent of the nation's total manufacturing effort takes place in Victoria. Of the State's 1.8 million wage-earners, nearly half a million are employed in manufacturing industries. Victoria is Australia's largest maker of butter and cheese, and biggest producer of canned meat and fruit while heavy industries like aluminium smelting, oil refining and petrochemical production are also largely based in Victoria.

As a result of its manufacturing base and central location, the nation's most intensively trafficked and best serviced domestic trade routes run through Victoria — rail, road and sea — and it is a focal point for international trade transport, too. Melbourne's road freight tonnage is a third bigger than in Sydney, showing the importance of its location as a crossroads for commercial production moving through, in and out of the country. Port Melbourne is the largest general cargo port in Australia and the biggest container terminal in the southern hemisphere. Sydney's airports handle half the level of domestic traffic moving through Melbourne's three airports: Tullamarine International, Essenden and

Moorabbin. Tullamarine is Australia's only 24-hour-a-day, 7-day-a-week commercial and cargo international airport.

Victoria has one of the most heavily protected manufacturing workforces in Australia, and union interests remain prominent: for Victoria is as much a base for Australia's union might as it is for the 'old money' employers. In recent years, to assist 'rationalisation' of industries and stem further job losses, the State Government has responded with financial, technological and planning assistance for businesses struggling to survive or those looking for new markets. Yet the economic direction will remain in manufacturing, say the experts, due to its roots in processing of farm goods and energy resources, as well as physical limitations for a state with only 3 per cent of the continent's land.

Due to its small size and dense, well-established population, people who move to Victoria can expect better access to consumer goods and services than in the other larger, newer states.

Favoured projects in Victoria

As far as attracting immigrants and foreign investors, the State Government is clear about the types of projects it considers favourable to the economy. Applicants whose proposed businesses fall into the following categories are actively encouraged by the State Government:

- advanced materials
- agricultural chemicals
- biotechnology
- measurement
- mineral processing
- mineral exploration
- environment monitoring
- pharmaceuticals
- biotechnology and food production generally
- computer technology involving hardware, software and communication standards

Specific assistance to new or developing enterprises is provided through the **Victorian Economic Development Corporation**; it has a charter to facilitate and encourage balanced industrial development, investment and technology from abroad and interstate, and to upgrade tourist facilities and the export of goods and services. Victoria aims a financial assistance programme at medium and small enterprises which can show their potential for growth through additional funding. To be eligible, companies must present a strategy or **business plan**. Their case for funding may be based on a need to compete against imports or move into new markets. They must also show that the level of help they require is not beyond the Government's existing levels of protection normal for such industries, nor must their expansion cause similar enterprises in Victoria to suffer. A business in any area of manufacturing can seek Government assistance if it proposes to expand or introduce its products into foreign markets. The State may help pay for research and development of new products and markets, participation in exhibitions and tender-bidding abroad as well as strategic business planning so the venture can raise capital from the private finance market.

The State is willing to tailor an assistance package to each applicant on merit. Generally, assistance will be through loans and loan guarantees, equity participation in a perceived growth area or through grants. Winning a grant relies on evidence by an applicant that the proposed business would be in an area of 'significance' and rapid growth as well as creating jobs.

Government incentives and assistance for large or publicly listed companies, and those outside the programme for manufacturing concerns, are also available. Foreign companies seeking to locate in Victoria may also be eligible. Such aid is usually conditional on the company reaching a certain target through a **performance agreement** — making this very much a normal commercial deal with the State. The company may be obliged to enter into 'appropriate consultative arrangements' with its workforce and trade unions. In addition to these loan and grant incentives to private enterprise, Victoria offers help to companies planning to decentralise by moving to locations where there are job shortages or other possibilities for growth. The Government's **regional development strategy** defines areas and policies for provision of jobs, housing, social and general infrastructure and town planning outside Melbourne and major industrial or commercial centres.

Further Information
Department of Industry, Technology and Resources, 228 Victoria Parade, East Melbourne, Victoria, 3002. The State Government also has representatives in Frankfurt, London, Tokyo and Los Angeles. Or contact the nearest Australian High Commission, Embassy or Trade Commission.

NEW SOUTH WALES

New South Wales is Australia's oldest, richest and most heavily populated State. Of its 5.4 million people, three quarters live on the coast and 3.4 million in Sydney. Sydney is said by its fans to be the most spectacular urban environment in the world. Its famous harbour foreshores and lush, hillside suburbs are breathtakingly beautiful. The majestic, glittering water views from many and varied vantage points, semi-tropical vegetation, huge houses and apartments with sweeping panoramas of the city, set on private beaches or in huge bush gardens, make Sydney as beautiful an environment as anywhere on earth for city living. Many suburban streets are, literally, on a waterway or beach — be it ocean, harbour or riverside.

Sydney is one of the biggest cities in the world, extending 50km to the north, south, and west of the harbour, where its commercial and historical centre lies. Nearby centres like Wollonging to the south, Gosford to the north and towns of the Blue Mountains in the west are virtually part of greater Sydney and have similar landscapes and lush climates. On the other hand, Sydney's suburbs are often grimy, flat, hot, and monotonous and several hours' driving time through heavy traffic from a reasonable beach or picnic spot. Summer time can bring health hazards like water pollution; some of southern Sydney's surf beaches emit an unpleasant stench and are regularly closed to swimmers.

Out and about in NSW

Elsewhere, New South Wales is a large rugged State. It has a number of green belts along the coast and major rivers, as well as many historic, colonial towns which live — or have died — with booms in farming or mining. Like Queensland and Victoria, the climates of New South Wales have the variety of a whole continent. There are snowy mountains (and Australia's highest, Mount Koscuisko, 2,228 metres above sea level) for skiing in winter, semi-tropical lakes, rivers, rain forest and coastal stretches in the north, desert in the far west, millions of acres of flat farmland and bushland as well.

Sydney as a Financial Centre

New South Wales generates more than a third of the nation's Gross National Product and Sydney is recognised as one of the most important financial growth centres in the Pacific region. The Reserve Bank of Australia is headquartered in Sydney, as are more than half of Australia's 200 most profitable companies, according to the way the State Government juggles its statistics (as a variation on a claim made by the Victorian government). Sydney's impressive modern Stock Exchange building has more companies listed on it than the exchanges of Melbourne or Perth and half Australia's total share turnover; and it's the only local exchange maintaining a market in call options. Sydney's nearby Futures Exchange is the only one which deals in gold, wool, meat, export beef and interest rates. There is also a foreign exchange hedge market covering market risks.

Manufacturing in NSW

The State provides about 40 per cent of the nation's total employment and the same proportion of its manufacturing output. It manufactures goods from food, beverages, tobacco, textiles, footwear and clothing through to fabricated metals. It has three oil refineries and more than 30 petrochemical plants.

New South Wales is the biggest steel producer in the country — some 80 per cent of the national annual output — as well as being Australia's leading producer of wheat, wool and poultry goods and ranking second to Queensland in beef production.

Coal is the State's main mineral resource. It also has significant reserves of silver, copper, zinc, lead, tin, titanium and rutile. Government policy has aimed at building up the State's electricity supply for industrial purposes by the 1990s and natural gas as well as hydro-electric schemes provide its present power supply for domestic and commercial purposes.

However, NSW has experienced a swing away from manufacturing and mining activities to investment in services and high technology from the middle 1980s. At the start of the decade, this sector accounted for only 15 per cent of all investment but now represents more than two thirds of all new projects. Mining and manufacturing have declined from a 40 per cent share of investment activity to 15 per cent. Local authorities encourage siting for **advanced technology parks** (where such enterprises share industrial or office sites) and service industries. Sydney is now a centre for a highly competitive computer industry.

Typically, this State Government is protectionist in policy to large employers, propping them up even though they remain in a less buoyant sector of the economy. But despite changes in economic patterns due to recession and high interest rates, the number of self-employed people in New South Wales has grown markedly — up nearly 45 per cent in the two years to September 1985. The number of small businesses employing under 100 people rose 20 per cent in the same period.

About 30 per cent of Australia's business migrants settle in New South Wales, mainly in Sydney. They come mostly from Britain, North America, the Middle East, Africa, Hong Kong and Taiwan.

Business incentives

The State provides a range of business programmes and incentives to newcomers and established residents, to help them with investment or business expansion plans. These are generally administered by the **NSW Investment Corporation**. Specific private or public sector proposals are considered for assistance on the basis of likely contribution to employment and economic development. At its international offices, the State Government maintains investment and trade advisory services to assist organisations and would-be immigrants set up joint ventures, arrange licensing agreements, and the exchange or sale of technology as well as the establishment of operations in Australia. The State provides individual counselling and step-by-step guides through the morass of red tape a suitable business migrant will encounter on lodging a **Statement of Intent** with national migration officials and in seeking permission to set up in New South Wales.

The NSW Investment Corporation also provides help with raising loans and funds. Grants may be made to eligible businesses in this perceived growth area of the economy. NSWIC can guarantee loans or provide funds in conjunction with private banks or investors. Such finance can be used to cover commercialisation of innovative products or processes, including final development, prototype, production start-up and initial marketing phases. Working capital can also be used for expansion of new technology enterprises and introduction of innovative techniques or equipment to improve efficiency. The Government runs an **Advanced Technology Centre** giving free information and advice to business, such as on possible locations and venture capital.

Proposals for assistance stand the best chance if they fall into one of the following categories:

- advanced industrial processes
- advanced electronic systems including computer hardware and office equipment
- communications technology
- biomedical, medical and pharmaceutical technology
- new energy systems including laser technology

- new materials technology
- new transportation and materials handling technologies
- computer software and systems analysis

Decentralisation of industry is another facet of New South Wales's incentives to existing business as well as investors from outside. The offers aim to compensate for the additional costs of locating and transporting goods outside the Sydney region. Payroll tax rebates of up to 100 per cent to approved manufacturers and processors, and offers of loans and guarantees for land, factory premises and machinery have been part of the NSW government policy for encouraging new business. Often a local government in that area will offer incentives to the business as well, including help with finance for the project.

Housing assistance like rent subsidies or loans to cover construction of homes for employees at the new site may also be part of the package as well as **subsidies** for costs of removing machinery to the regional location. Subsidies to meet consultancy services for the project (if these services can help solve operational, productivity, and/or profitability problems) may also be available from the Government. Help in meeting fees charged by consultant designers who work on an approved industrial project has also been offered via the NSW Government in the past, while it gives preference to eligible regional manufacturers when allocating Government contracts.

Further Information
New South Wales Investment Corporation, 8-18 Bent Street, Sydney, NSW 2000. The New South Wales Government also has official representatives in London, Tokyo, and Los Angeles. Or contact the nearest Australian High Commission, Embassy or Trade Commission.

TASMANIA

The heart-shaped island to the south of Australia's mainland often gets left off the map altogether, much to the irritation of Tasmanians. Yet it is a real jewel: green, mountainous, and unpolluted. The island continent's island State is said by health freaks, conservationists, farmers and suburbanites already there to be the world's finest place for a wholesome lifestyle, safe from the horrifying effects of nuclear accident or war.

"I am always building veritable castles in the air about emigrating, and Tasmania has been my headquarters of late," wrote Charles Darwin back in 1854...and today's nature lovers may also do well to consider a move to Tasmania. However, it is isolated from the mainland by the Bass

Strait which, despite considerable transport subsidies to help the island's trade and commerce, is said to be its major drawback.

A tiny population — less than half a million people — means the state has limited potential if making a lot of money is a crucial factor in planning your change of lifestyle. Australians from the mainland in the north joke about in-breeding due to a shortage of people, claiming that the Tasmanians have two heads arising from genetic weaknesses, and so forth. Naturally, jests of this sort gall the island's inhabitants. Indeed, the main towns of Hobart and Launceston in particular are very cosmopolitan. As well as the British who settled what was for its first 70 years a notoriously barbaric prison colony known as Van Dieman's Land — Tasmania's main ethnic groups are of Mediterranean, East European and Dutch origin.

True, the outlook of many Tasmanians tends to be parochial. But such is the price paid by a population in close touch with an environment often more verdant, rolling, neat, civilized and 'English' than rural England. Even in Hobart, the capital city, locals buy seafood fresh from trawlers at the docks — whereas in other urban centres of mainland Australia and many Western countries people may not see fish before it is gutted and presented in a foam dish on the supermarket shelf.

Tasmania has been referred to as the 'sanitorium of tropical Australia'. So, if you favour a spacious, relaxed environment of forests and lakes, without extremes in temperature, and you can do without a wide range of organised entertainments and indoor culture, Tasmania's easy-going style could represent Utopia.

Though the average income of Tasmania's population is relatively low, so too are the prices of goods and services which make up the cost of living. Property is easier and cheaper to rent or buy than in more crowded, commercial places in Australia; even the biggest city, Hobart, has only 170,000 people. In peak hour it takes just half an hour to traverse Hobart by car from its farthest suburb to the centre.

Public policy

Like the States with 'left-wing' administrations in recent years, the fact that so-called 'right-wingers' of the Liberal Party have run Tasmania for most of the 1980s makes little difference in terms of economic and social policies. In Tasmania, perhaps more than elsewhere, the two main political parties battle it out to claim the middle ground as their own — the Labor Party sticking with the would-be dam-builders and developers on major environmental issues.

The problem of ecology versus economics is of interest to most Tasmanians. On one hand, their State is famous for its bushland and big rivers, boasting the last temperate wilderness on earth; a third of the

State is locked up in national parks and other conservation areas. Yet environmental problems arise with the notion of exploiting available land for the woodchip industries and mining. Tasmania's Hydro-Electric Commission, an autonomous semi-government body, is the single most powerful political force on the island. HEC interests clash with those of 'greenie' pressure groups, and never more than in the row of the early 1980s over the HEC's determination to dam the Franklin River in order to add to the existing 23 power stations feeding over 7,000 million kilowatt hours already in its grid. The debate became an international battle which resulted in this river being listed as a World Heritage area to protect it from dam-builders. The controversy put Tasmania on the world tourist map. Rafting down the Franklin or other wild rivers of Tasmania is a popular holiday pursuit for mainlanders and foreign tourists. Partly due to the attention the Tasmanian wilderness achieved through the controversy over the Franklin, tourism could be worth more to the economy than more hydro-electric power for industries which do not yet exist — or so the 'greenies' claim.

Tasmanian tourism
Tourism is bringing in record numbers of people. Would-be immigrants who work in the catering or hospitality sectors could do well in a State with high unemployment and limited prospects in retail and service industries. Indeed, its schools were the first in Australia to offer tourism as a subject for study and tourism courses at the State's colleges of further educational are well-established.

Industrial development
Tin and iron are major mineral exports, and aluminium smelting a big processing industry. The effort to attract heavy industry to Tasmania through subsidised transport to compensate for distances from markets and mainland ports, has been successful with the opening of Australia's first silicon factory south of Hobart. In the 1980s new aquaculture ventures like oyster, trout, abalone, scallop and Atlantic salmon farming started up, helping to increase employment by 4.6 per cent a year by 1987, about twice Australia's national average.

Other innovations include extraction and export of natural chemicals and essential oils of such plants as boronia, peppermint, spearmint and caraway. Considering its small size and population, Tasmania's small-scale export industries are diverse and successful: finding a market for cheeses in Japan, sporting rifles in the United States, passenger catamarans and computer software in Europe and — would you believe — prefabricated igloos in Antarctica.

Like the other States and Territories of Australia, Tasmania specifies 'economic diversification', 'hi-tech' and 'manufacturing' sectors as the keys to continuing prosperity and economic expansion. It is keen to develop processing and manufacturing ventures based on its sea and land farming. To this end, the **Tasmanian Development Authority** was set up in 1983 to guide and encourage new business and investment. The presence of a large available workforce with low incidence of strikes and other union disruptions is emphasised in making the case for relocating in Tasmania. Prospective business migrants and foreign investors are invited to approach the Tasmanian Development Authority with their proposals. Run by prominent local businesspeople, the Authority is now one of the most influential bodies in the nation, in terms of how it can determine Government decisions and invest public money in private enterprise.

The Authority is empowered to

● acquire, develop and dispose of land for business undertakings
● make grants for research and development as well as the expansion of businesses
● acquire an interest in any business considered significant to the State's development
● be represented on governing bodies of the businesses it assists
● create business co-operatives
● engage consultants and independent contractors and establish advisory committees
● provide business advice and technical assistance

It also provides marketing and sales support material at interstate and international trade fairs and makes contact on behalf of Tasmania andits individual business ventures which may help to identify and win new markets.

The TDA has established a Primary Industry Finance Divison to encourage growth and innovation among farmers and other businesspeople in certain areas. It may approve ventures for which research has been completed but which are in need of money to pilot a new product or process. If research and trial phases are complete, the Finance Division may help an eligible business proceed to commercial production. The Authority can help industries with cheap loans and grants for approved agricultural products.

Further Information
Tasmanian Development Authority, 134 Macquarie Street, Hobart 7000, Tasmania. Or contact the nearest Australian High Commission, Embassy or Trade Commission.

CANBERRA AND THE AUSTRALIAN CAPITAL TERRITORY

Canberra is the city of dippos (diplomats), journos and pollies — the bush capital which thrives on hot air. As the hub of Australian politics, where the powerful and their pen-pushers congregate to run the country, it can be one of the most invigorating places in Australia. Canberra is where political, business, legal, cultural and diplomatic leaders find a home-from-home, the major national venue for what *blasé* insiders term 'gabfests'. It is also a mecca for academics and athletic stars, as home of both the Australian National University and the Institute of Sport. International artists and arty films show regularly at a variety of clubs, theatres and cinemas.

Life in Canberra
Though amid Australia's dusty green bush, Canberra is more like a vast country garden, a blaze of seasonal colour in springtime and autumn, for it is planted with 12 million trees, many of them imported from Europe. Canberra and its environs are studded with parkland picnic settings. Windsurfing and sailing on its central lake, swimming in nearby rivers or a two-hour drive to the georgeous beaches of the NSW south coast make free time a dream. It's only four hours down the expressway to Sydney, and you can shoot through to Melbourne in a day.

Canberra's public architecture is splendid. It has restaurants and international hotels out of all proportion to its population of 265,000. For the presence of the Australian parliament makes Canberra a privileged showpiece, Australia's Geneva, a Washington DC for Down Under.

Canberra can also be one of the most boring places to live and work in Australia — especially if you have no job at all. Nearly two-thirds of Canberra's workers are employed in the **Commonwealth Public Service** and, as consumers, its citizens are the best paid per capita in Australia; but youth unemployment is consistently high. Ironically, those who grow up there have access to some of the best education and sporting facilities in the land. Yet they are often forced to leave this one-industry town if they cannot get work with the public service, which is regularly 'pruned' and sniped at by successive governments eager to prove they are cutting public spending. Canberra's social life has neither the hedonism and flirtation of places like Sydney nor the cultural commitment of Melbourne, say its detractors. People ask: "*Who* are you?" — and follow-up with: "Who d'ya work for?"

Housing is as expensive as Melbourne's, making it more costly than in any big Australian city except Sydney, while the commercial property market is also tight compared to other capitals. On top of such drawbacks, people who run Canberra usually live somewhere else. For it is administered essentially at the whim of current members of the national parliament via the Commonwealth Public Service, with some input from a locally elected Advisory Council.

Canberra's origins

Canberra was founded in 1911, ten years after the various colonies of Australia became an independent federation; this followed a *fracas* involving bids by both Sydney and Melbourne to become the permanent seat of national government. An area of 911 square miles (2,359 square kilometres, about the size of Luxembourg) was granted by the State of New South Wales for the new Capital Territory. Previously, it was the site of a former sheep station known for nearly a century before as Canberry, a name derived by the station owner from an aboriginal word which, by chance, meant 'meeting place'.

A Chicago architect, Walter Burley Griffin, won a competition to design the model city. He included the concept of a large artificial lake in its centre and a number of widely separated satellite towns on roads radiating from the official Government heartland of the town. Though some find Canberra's circuits and circles frustrating to navigate, it is one of the more sensibly planned of Australia's urban environments. Green spaces divide its widely-spaced streets and buildings; there are restrictions against such eyesores as domestic fences; shops and offices are allocated to particular sections so that residential and recreation areas are undisturbed; while industry is strictly confined to three industrial estates.

Canberra business life

As the centre of national Government, more than 60 foreign embassies and major business lobby groups, the national and international banking community, accountancy and legal firms are well represented in Canberra.

The Australian National University, set on a huge, well-planned residential campus, attracts students from all over the world and provides a particularly pleasing environment for study and research. Both nourishing and feeding Canberra's university community are important quasi-academic government bodies, like the Australian Bureau of Statistics, and the Commonwealth Scientific and Industrial Research Organisation. These also attract high technology and computer industries to Canberra.

Naturally, many of the most lucrative contracts arise from Government work. Departments of social services, taxation and defence projects all rely increasingly on computerised gizmos to perform their functions.

The **Canberra Development Board,** consisting of private individuals and Government members appointed by the Minister for Territories, promotes private enterprise development in the ACT. It identifies projects which marry commerce with new technology as most suitable for the area, along with tourism. All these must have no polluting side-effects. Due to the proximity of both possible customers and employable expertise from the pool of skilled people already in Government or semi-government jobs, Canberra could be an attractive place for new business ventures, or expanding established projects, according to experts on the Board.

Alternatively, individuals with relevant training or experience in such industries may also find their niche in the Australian Capital Territory. Catering and restaurants are disproportionately important to the local economy. Since Australia's leaders, bosses, and media like to mix business with pleasure — new taxes on business entertainment notwithstanding — Canberra has a glut of establishments for wining and dining. On a good night, its up-market discos and international hotels are crammed with more grey suits than a bankers' convention — which is probably where everyone was anyway before they hit the dance floor. There are a number of elite clubs with excellent entertainment and restaurant facilities, as well as the obligatory leagues and 'footy' clubs both in the ACT and across the border in the NSW town of Queanbeyan, with vast halls of culture (ie poker machines).

Tourism

More than 3 million tourists visit the ACT each year, presenting a relatively recent burst of commercial opportunities for Canberrans. By the mid-1980s, tourism was earning the Territory some $A200 million a year and employed 6,500 people. With the opening of each impressive new building — the High Court, National Gallery, National Library, the Telecom Tower and of course the new Parliament House — more tourists put Canberra in the 'must see' category. Its closeness to Sydney and Melbourne, via a route which takes visitors through a variety of typical Aussie townships and scenery, adds to the attractions of a Canberra stopover.

Trade in the ACT

The high disposable incomes of many of Canberra's full or part-time residents also mean opportunities in the retail and consumer goods sector of the local economy. However, the spending power and number of people living in Canberra ebbs and flows with the size of the bureaucracy. In the early 1970s, under the Whitlam Labor Government, expansion plans forged ahead along with projects for vast modern shopping complexes, Government offices and housing for a bigger public service. Yet, by the time many of these buildings were ready for occupation, the more deflationary Liberal-National Country Party Government of Malcolm Fraser was in power, and cut back on public service staff ceilings. By the mid-1980s a different (Labor) Government meant slight expansion in the public service and bigger spending policies in certain sectors. Much of the slack in new housing, offices and retail centres was taken up, with richer pickings for shopkeepers and their business associates.

The Canberra Development Board also argues Canberra is a good place to locate since it is close to the richest consumer markets in the country — Sydney and the central coast of NSW — and lies halfway to Victoria and South Australia's domestic markets and international ports. As the biggest city in the NSW southern region, Canberra is already a business centre for boat-building, shoe-manufacturing, fish-canning, textile-manufacturing, milk-processing and steel-fabrication from nearby parts of NSW where such heavy industries are permitted. Conversely, the south coast region of NSW does well out of its accessibility from Canberra. At weekends and holidays the national capital's well-heeled residents make a mass exodus to the nearest beaches and campsites while many build their holiday homes in the tourist-oriented seaside towns.

Incentives

In the past there were incentives such as the absence of land taxes or financial institutions' duties, reflected in the fact that many businesses operating outside the ACT registered in the ACT; but these taxes have now been imposed. The Canberra Development Board however offers a range of other incentives and services to prospective business projects. Eligible ventures may qualify for loans and grants, and businesses which generate employment are favoured. Incentives include:

- subsidies to pay for up to half the cost of feasibility studies, within certain financial limits (up to $A20,000, at the time of writing)
- a maximum of 12 months' rental assistance towards housing of 25 per cent of key personnel
- rebates in payroll tax
- rebates for research and development staff or consultants engaged in approved projects for up to five years
- Government guarantees of loans up to 40 per cent of borrowing (maximum $A100,000 at the time of writing)
- exemptions in certain cases for municipal rates for up to five years

- capital assistance for land, buildings, plant and equipment (up to $A200,000 at the time of writing
- assistance in the construction of special development projects

Further Information
Canberra Development Board, GPO Box 938, Civic Square, Canberra ACT 2608, or contact the nearest Australian High Commission, Embassy or Trade Commission.

NORTHERN TERRITORY

"The Northern Territory is more than a land of contrasts...It's a spiritual experience." Well, it's hard to resist a giggle at this seemingly overblown sentiment in the Territory Government's official literature about the attractions of Australia's least populated, most undeveloped and rugged of terrains. Until you go there. Contrast the promotional blurb to the reaction of people who've actually experienced the staggering beauty and mystical quality for the first time. From atop Ayers Rock, in the dead heart of Australia, strangers have likened the experience to feeling 'as if my head has been lifted off and changed for a new one.'

Old-timers may say too many 'Darwin Stubbies' (large bottles of beer) contribute to the heady mixture of tropical and desert environment in the Northern Territory. The vast distances between its few townships are measured by the amount of beer you'll need for the journey. A six-pack from Tennant Creek to Alice, locals might drawl, meaning it's a hot desert drive of 505 km, about 300 miles.

Those too young for beer feel the impact of the environment another way, even if of 'non-Aboriginal' origin. At a mixed race school in the outback, the story goes, a teacher asked children to draw their self-portraits. Many handed in landscapes with trees, rocks, rivers and gullies — no human faces.

The Northern Territory's overall style is informal, to say the least. Aboriginals remain the poor relatives of the rest of the population, somehow slipping through the nets of various government programmes to 'help them help themselves'. The locals, as well as immigrants who have come to live and work in the Northern Territory, often dismiss the 30,000-odd Aboriginals (a quarter of the NT's population) as a bunch of lazy drunks and no-hopers, unable to understand why they have not cashed in on 'civilisation'.

As in most Australian mining towns, the going is rough, tough and macho. At present, the richest mining activities are the extraction of gold, copper, tin, tantalite, wolfram and huge deposits of uranium, manganese and bauxite. After mining, tourism and beef cattle are the most prominent commercial activities. Wave Hill Station is Australia's biggest cattle ranch, all 12,380 square km (4,780 square miles) of it.

Darwin
The Territory's capital is Darwin, founded in the 1860s and flattened by Cyclone Tracy in 1974. Now a low-rise modern sprawl, it has the hottest average temperatures in Australia for both summer and winter (average maximum in January at 31.7°C, average maximum in July 30.3°C). Rather than hot and cold, Darwin's weather pattern is wet or dry. Either way, it has a higher average for sunshine than any other Australian capital, at 8.5 hours daily. It also has the smallest number of people, about 65,000.

The population of the entire NT is also the most sparse, around 140,000, though it is the third biggest State in area after Western Australia and Queensland. The average age of its people is strikingly low — at 24 — and 80 per cent of the population is under 40.

Public policy
It became self-governing (within the federation) in 1978, and is governed along slightly different lines from other States with a Chief Minister not a Premier, and an Adminstrator not a Governor. Politically the mood is macho-cowboy, with strong sympathies for the tough rightist style of Queensland's National Party administration over the border within the NT's predominantly Country-Liberal Party Government (a single party rather than a coalition of Nationals and Liberals as in other places).

There are ongoing rows over ecology versus economics; the conservationists are usually spoken for by non-Territorians who want to stop uranium mining and protect wildlife areas like Kakadu National Park, which already has World Heritage Listing for environmental protection. Since tourism comes second to mining as the NT's biggest source of income and employment, the question mark over exploiting the environment looms ever larger. Safari-style holidays, casinos in Darwin and Alice Springs, and major construction of luxurious 'villages' to accommodate half a million visitors a year exemplify the benefits of tourism. Its major developments and investments are sited in or near prime attractions, such as the Olgas, stone remains of an ancient, long-buried mountain range, and of course the biggest boulder in the world, Ayers Rock.

Business and industry
More than anywhere in Australia, the Northern Territory needs businesspeople with ideas and capital to invest in development. The land

is concentrated in relatively few hands, while a handful of large public mining companies are the biggest employers in a lop-sided economy.

But being closer to South-East Asian capitals than to consumer markets in Sydney or Melbourne, Darwin and its port is well-sited for export and trade. This port, one of Australia's largest, is constantly being upgraded for development of further international shipping links, while Darwin's airport is being redeveloped to meet the needs of a larger, more sophisticated clientele. The Territory Government is also pushing ahead with plans to seal more outback roads and so improve internal transport, since internal airfares in Australia are high; a railway to link Alice Springs with Darwin 1,482km (1,000 miles) away has also been proposed. In February 1987, the entire road from Adelaide in South Australia to Darwin, 3,000 km due north through Australia's dead centre, was finally sealed and opened to heavy duty road traffic. Sealing with bitumen the entire stretch of Stuart Highway linking the two capitals was described by the Federal Government (which paid for it) as the single biggest engineering achievement Australians have ever undertaken.

Due to plentiful mineral resources and natural power the NT can now cater for medium-scale steel fabrication, earth-moving, electrical and structural engineering projects which could be useful in developing the State's infrastructure for future trade and industry. A number of international traders have moved into Darwin during the 1980s, lured by its new facilities and closeness to giant markets in the Asian region, particularly.

Incentives

Since the economy is a baby in terms of the rest of Australia, its economic planners are basic and open-minded in matters of planning permission and Government incentives. The Northern Territory Government aims to encourage growth in private sector investment generally. Mining, processing and export of its livestock and fishing produce, and of course capitalising on the flood of tourists who want to see the Top End for themselves are defined by the Government as desirable for development and investment. Economic diversification through manufacturing or business services is also encouraged.

Incentives to new investment depend on the individual project, and are decided in each case by the Territory's industry experts. The Government has established a **Trade Development Zone Authority** to create investment opportunities in manufacturing. Sales tax, customs and excise duty incentives and exemptions are available to eligible businesses. The Authority's area of influence is in ventures which are export and manufacturing trade-oriented. **Nortrade** is another government body which can help newcomers plan and realise export or import-oriented ventures.

The Department of Business, Technology and Communications declares that the overall thrust of any grants, loans or incentives to business is for the promotion, expansion and development of secondary and tertiary industry. It is *not* promising barrels of money in grants. Rather, with input from Nortrade it works to identify gaps in various markets, particularly in Asia. At home, the Department aims to identify potential for new and expanded enterprises and encourage investment from local, interstate and overseas sources. Incentives and advice are available to business of all sizes, and there is a specific interest in encouraging small ventures to put down roots in the Territory.

Further Information
Nortrade, GPO Box 2245, Darwin 5794, North Territory. Also: Department of Business, Technology and Communications, GPO Box 2056, Darwin, Northern Territory. Or contact the nearest Australian High Commission, Embassy or Trade Commission.

WESTERN AUSTRALIA

The so-called 'wild west' of Australia is said to be the best place in the country for people with millionaire potential. The people of Perth and the green, buzzing south-east corner of Western Australia are making waves on national and international markets with their ambition and showmanship. However, the millionaire yachtie way of life — portrayed as 'average' for West Australians in the wake of the America's Cup challenge in 1987 — is misleading. Though about two-thirds of Australia's largest State's 1.5 million people are concentrated in slick, cosmpolitan Perth and its satellite towns, WA's far-flung mining and farm communities are another world.

Even Australians brought up in the cities can be shocked by the cowboys and miners when they venture through the stunted outback terrain to mining communities.

As one 'Easterner', fresh from a university course in Melbourne, wrote back to his family during a holiday mining job: "Meekatharra is a typical outback Australian town. I think some of the people I have seen in its Royal Mail hotel were extras in [Paul Hogan's movie] *Crocodile Dundee*. Out of the three times I have been in the pub, I have witnessed two brawls. It is totally different from the East. The pub which the Aborigines frequent is referred to as the 'coon pub'...I have spent most days out with the drilling rigs taking soil samples etc. It is quite interesting as we are working around a lot of old sites — mine shafts that were in operation around the turn of the century. To be a driller, I think you must have to pass a word speed test. If you can say 'f—' ten times within the space of sixty seconds of normal conversation, it must help." Hugh Berryman of Melbourne, in a letter to the author, October 1986.

However, those heavy drinking, hard swearing blokes at work extracting various ores from the ground are highly paid to compensate for the isolation from women, children and the comforts of the suburbs thousands of kilometres distant.

Mining and sales of minerals as well as export of agricultural goods are the foundations of the State's economy. Western Australia and Queensland together represent the mainstay of the nation's income from overseas trade. Like Queensland, Western Australia is eagerly developing its natural resources. Huge investments have been made in the North-West Shelf gas project as well as new mineral developments and downstream processing. Major export commodities include iron ore, nickel, mineral sands, salt, alumina, meat, wool and wheat. The State's port and road infrastructures are well-established and crucial to stoking the demand of key customers — the biggest being Japan and the United States.

However, foreign markets are fickle, as the plummeting commodity prices of the mid-70s showed. The recent history of the State's biggest export commodity, iron ore, illuminates the point: during a boom in demand from Japan's steel industry in the 1960s, Western Australia was well-positioned geographically and in terms of resources to supply this apparently wonderful market. But the world recession caused a fall in demand and prices for steel and, consequently, iron ore. Fortunately, the industry has recovered somewhat with new markets in Taiwan and South Korea. The unreliability of the needs and prices offered for raw materials and foodstuffs by its big customers in Asia and the US have forced Government and business to look to technology, financial services, processing and manufacturing to generate WA's future wealth. Nevertheless, much of Western Australia's business activity still flows from huge farming, mining and export efforts, so commercial and manufacturing sectors remain another kind of goldmine for people in WA.

However, its main commercial centres are enjoying a burst of activity due to rapid population growth, mainy through migration. Over 50 per cent more people lived in WA in 1981 than in 1966 — yet population growth for Australia as a whole was only 29 per cent in the same period. Isolation from the better-established Eastern consumer markets across the continent also presents many opportunities for newcomers with skills and ideas.

Expertise in mining, dry land farming, prevention of soil erosion are sold to clients around the world by entrepreneurs from Western Australia. More tangible items, like beer and machinery for mining and farming, are made and marketed by Western Australians to customers at home and overseas. Western Australia's Labor Government publishes more promotional literature to attract investors and businessfolk than any other State or Territory. People who might be tempted to set up shop in WA could spend a whole week reading about its economic potential and progress in its industrial and commercial sectors. The Government produces jolly statistics showing that growth in employment, production and trade are well ahead of averages for the rest of the country. It also identifies areas of perceived growth and opportunity for migrants...right down to costings for running a sheep station, for example.

Though Perth's stock exchange is smaller than that of Sydney or Melbourne, it boasts the highest growth rate in terms of new companies listed; it also has a second board market, raising venture capital for new businesses. State officials in charge of encouraging foreign investors and business migrants naturally point to the high proportion of millionaires and people making 'new money', most prominent and powerful among them being Perth's golden-boy migrants, Alan Bond — once a Londoner, and Robert Holmes à Court — originally from Rhodesia.

The **West Australian Development Corporation** was established to promote economic activity in the state. Meanwhile, the Western Australian **Exim Corporation** aims to aid export-oriented ventures, with a network of overseas contacts to act as agents and distributors for locally manufactured products and services. Exim also supplies a range of investment advisory and agency services to potential foreign investors. New industries may apply to the State's **Technology Development Authority** for grants and loans from the Technology Development Fund towards such costs as preparation of business plans and product refinement. Through the fund, equity investment is also available (up to $A500,000 at the time of writing) for new technology-based businesses deemed to be of benefit to the State's industrial development.

Western Australia is also keen on financial services. Foreign banks are encouraged to base themselves in Perth rather than, with most of Australia's financial institutions, in Melbourne or Sydney. The State Government has also given the go-ahead for the nation's first International Insurance Exchange — along the lines of Lloyds of London and North American insurance exchanges — expected to be operating by January 1988. Due to its proximity to South East Asia and being in a similar time zone to major users in the western Pacific rim, Perth is promoted as an ideal base for such a self-governing exchange to offer trade and associated facilities.

The **Small Business Development Corporation** has also been set up by the State Government to offer information and advice to small and medium businesses. It holds training seminars and workshops both in city and selected country areas.

The State has a range of incentives to develop tourism, since this is predicted by economic experts to become one of its biggest moneyspinners by the 1990s. The **Western Australian Tourist Commission** is, like those of other States, encouraged by the recent influx of foreign holidaymakers and adventurers to Australia. But unlike the east coast, tourism is a relatively new business for WA. Perth at least is on the tourist map now, what with the America's Cup challenge, the Australian Bicentenary in 1988, and all that hype about champagne in every glass and a millionaire in every mansion.

The Government may also guarantee loans for tourism projects but the applicants must arrange and obtain the loan themselves. However, the Tourist Commission will give advice on possible sources for finance and may offer to buy equity in ventures. It may arrange to subscribe for or otherwise buy and sell shares in a private company; it may exercise a right to appoint a director to its board, in exchange for providing money for a project. Selected developers and investors may even benefit from familiarisation trips, to show them the potential of a site for tourism. In cases where the government owns land it has earmarked for tourist development, it may decide to contribute the 'fair market value' of that property or provide loans for approved equity participants, in exchange for a share of the total completed value of the project.

Business migrants are offered advice and counselling on all aspects of operating a business in Western Australia by State Government offices overseas or by contacting its organisations directly, in Australia.

Immigration guidelines are interpreted and explained to indivduals. The State also offers to identify existing businesses in the State interested in joint ventures, technology transfer, manufacturing or licensing agreements which might be of interest to business migrants.

Further Information

WA Department of Resources Development, SGIO Atrium, 170 St George's Terrace, Perth 6000, Western Australia. The Western Australian government also has representatives in London and Tokyo. Or contact the nearest Australian High Commission, Embassy or Trade Commission.

8
Money and Making It

"Whaddya mean, noovo? I've been a millionaire for 20 years!"

That's how English emigré and Australian millionaire, Alan Bond, responded when acused of being *nouveau riche*. As Bond implies, once you've made that fortune in Austraila, considerable effort is required to keep it. His response also reflects how truly 'noovo' Australia is. Who cares how *long* you've had money, as long as you have it *now*!

Bond was 12 when he came to Australia with his family from the London suburb of Ealing on a £10 assisted passage. Today his interests in gold, beer (he makes half the amber fluid sold Down Under), yachting (which made him a national hero when he won the America's Cup for Perth in 1983), property, media...make him one of the best-known of his adopted country's 25,000 millionaires. Alan Bond-style achievement is a dream for many who'd like to go to Australia for work and play in future, or who play and work there already.

Of course, most people do *not* become captains of industry sailing their luxury yachts while the millions pile up. A blast of positive publicity in recent years adds to the impression that success comes easy and Australia is wide open to people with a few ideas about how to make money. But however easy the country may be to live in, finding a lucrative job or a good investment is a competitive business. The place is not paved with gold, diamonds, mining leases and brilliant contracts.

Nor should that leisurely local drawl fool you into believing that customers Down Under are a bunch of 'drongos' who don't know a 'bull artist' when they see one. Those thinking of going into business, using the incentive and support programmes offered by the various governments in Australia (detailed in Chapter 7, **Business Migration - Locations and Incentives**) should remember that the vast middle class has lately started to feel the pinch of economic recession. Craig and Craigette Consumer are not so easily persuaded to part with their (admittedly high) disposable wages on a whim.

If you hope to improve your income and job prospects in the move to

Australia, consider that unemployment levels are as high as in many other Western industrial societies (over 8 per cent in 1987). Inflation is double and even triple the rates of other Western countries, constantly nibbling at the edges of Australians' much-vaunted high disposable incomes. Employers, State and Federal Governments have lately been winning a battle to keep wage increases a couple of percentage points below the annual rate of inflation, just under 10 per cent. Rises in the cost of living are a constant worry for business, Government, and workers whose pay is being constantly eroded. A weak Australian dollar means the price of imports — luxuries and basics — spiral even higher. Despite recent measures like taxfree share dividends and a cut in the top income tax rate from 60 per cent to 49 per cent, individuals and companies all too easily find themselves in the top tax bracket anyway. A new capital gains tax, higher company rates and a clampdown on company perks adds to the pain. As realists like Alan Bond would confirm, those who do get rich in Australia work long and hard to stay that way. Reading between the lines of all this 'immigrant makes good' hype the message is clear; the potential for newcomers with expertise, goods and services is growing. Australians do like spending money on leisure and improving their lifestyles. Yet the recession makes for an increasingly rugged economic climate, while consumers at home and abroad grow ever more discerning.

ATTITUDES TO WORK

"Australian commercial bankers have a reputation as five o'clock boozers, particularly in London. The reputation has been earned over many years. They are remembered as very hail-fellow-well-met, and habitual openers of the drinks cabinet at five o'clock each weekday afternoon.
"The fact that this is no longer the case makes our reputation all the more a source for concern."

Thus saith Nicholas Whitlam, managing director of the State Bank of New South Wales about Aussie merchant bankers specifically — and many other Australian workers by implication. Whether bus drivers, accountants or the aforementioned bankers with comfy postings OS, working Aussies are generally portrayed as a soft lot — except when it comes to asking for more from grumbling management and governments.

Despite the over-indulged and strike-happy image, studies indicate that Australia's workforce in its much-maligned manufacturing industries is not particularly inefficient. Findings published in 1987 showed that Australian employees do not work less hard than those in factories of West Germany and Holland. Nor are their equipment and skills inferior.

Other industrial countries have healthier manufacturing sectors due to their 'absolute concentration on quality' by workers, the Government study found. Lack of quality products can be construed as a fault of Australian management, too. As this report tactfully states: "...there is an urgent need to accelerate the rate at which Australian industries adopt quality concepts...not only quality control but also original product design and manufacturing procedures."

STRIKES, UNIONS AND THE ACCORD

Australia's industrial climate is sporadically 'turbulent'. The most strike-torn year of the 1980s was 1981-82, with 4,192,000 working days lost in disputes. Even now, with relative peace on the union front, Australia is dogged by its reputation for strikes, especially in transport and mining industries, leading some overseas customers to look elsewhere for steady supplies of raw materials.

However, since 1983 an 'Accord' between Government, unions and business has managed to keep industrial harmony and even force drops in real wages. The Accord, while it lasts, limits union claims to pay and conditions, and employers' applications for price rises for key goods and services. The goal is to cut inflation, boost productivity and improve economic conditions generally. That's the high-minded philosophy, anyhow.

In reality all parties are engaged in a perpetual struggle to force someone else to agree to compromise on wages, working conditions, superannuation deals, prices, tax rates and Government-generated incentives. Arm-twisting in back rooms and fruity language in public remain a feature of industrial 'negotiations' between governments, unions and employers, Accord or no Accord. The future of this unique industrial policy depends on the Hawke administration staying in power, since the more politically right-wing opposition parties are committed to scrapping it.

Reflecting the key role of unions in Australian society, Prime Minister Bob Hawke was previously president of the Australian Council of Trade Unions (ACTU) for a decade. Repeated surveys show that Australians distrust the motives of trade unions, despite — or maybe due to — the fact that so many people belong to one or another. Unions are about as popular as politicans.

As around the world, trade unions and their activists are traditionally blamed for many economic problems by a media dominated by business interests. Yet, in most cases, trade union leaders and their aspirations are, like Australians themselves, middle class rather than militant. There are about 300 unions, representing more than half of Australia's workforce and making it one of the most unionised societies in the world.

Professional associations

The professions also have their associations. Though it is not always necessary to belong to one in order to practise, people in the professions find their incomes and code of ethics are often set by the official lobby group, which advises governments and industry tribunals on matters relating to people who practice in law, medicine, engineering and so forth. There are also a number of influential employer and industry groups at local, state and federal level playing a role in Australia's industrial system.

Disputes and claims

State arbitration courts and tribunals are responsible for settling disputes and administering claims for wages and conditions by the unions in different industries. Traditionally, the aim of governments (State and Federal, who may be represented at hearings) and employers is to keep 'real' wages below inflation, to keep prices competitive and avoid forcing a new round of application for rises in the costs of goods and services. Unions will often base arguments for a better deal on evidence that their members' earnings are being eroded by inflation, or in comparison with the deals given to other industries or unions. Bargaining in and out of the courts is the name of the industrial game; parties will often make 'ambit' claims — way in excess of what they actually expect to gain.

The **Conciliation and Arbitration Commission** is the highest legal authority within the Australian industrial system. It is an independent court established under a provision of the Australian Commonwealth constitution 'for the prevention and settlement of industrial disputes extending beyond the limits of any State'. It has played a leading political and economic role in recent years, making decisions on wage indexation. Indexation refers to the amount by which pay rates should rise, to take account of inflation. Under the Accord, employers, unions, the Government and other interested parties argue their points of view, then the judges make a decision. In 1987 the ruling was for maximum pay increases of 6.5 per cent — less than what unions asked for, but more than increases which business and Government advised. This indexation ruling kept pay about 3 percentage points less than the rate of inflation. Since the parties accepted it, it was considered proof that the above mentioned Accord between government, unions and business can continue to work.

If you are thinking of working in Australia, or becoming an employer in a particular industry, it may be wise to make contact with relevant trade union, professional or business organisations there. Unions are geared to provide advice and information in answer to questions about minimum rates of pay, working conditions, job prospects and preparation for any specific hurdles in setting up in Australia. Newcomers will find that many jobs require the people who take them to join the relevant trade union or association and pay their dues.

AWARDS AND CONDITIONS

Outsiders accustomed to less money and longer hours may drool at the idea that Australia's workers often earn high wages in comparison to the cost of living and have plenty of sunny holidays to enjoy on full pay plus 17.5 per cent 'loading'. Loading is a term which outsiders may not have heard before in reference to the pay packet. It means an additional portion of a worker's normal weekly salary added to the pay they receive when on holiday.

Similarly, a reference to 'award' is often made in Australia during discussions of the basic money and conditions workers may expect. As mentioned previously, awards are set by industrial courts at State or Federal level, and simply refer to the pay and conditions.

The regular indexation of pay packets to increase salaries in line with inflation and trade-offs against actual increases, like cuts in income taxes, deals to improve conditions, shorter hours, employer-paid superannuation and equal opportunities employment laws, are features of the working life in Australia. Compensation for injuries or accidents at work, superannuation schemes, and a reasonably efficient system of appeals through tribunals or other courts to which people can take complaints, add up to a good deal for the four million people in full-time jobs, and another three million who work part time or are self-employed.

Working hours
The standard working week throughout Australia is 40 hours but union awards typically set a 35 to 38 hour week. Overtime opportunities are well-paid with loadings or days off in lieu. Holidays are set at four to six weeks a year, depending on the industry, plus half a dozen public holidays. A week or two's sick leave on full pay is also part of the award for employees in many industries.

People higher on the corporate ladder and the self-employed work longer hours than the average worker, according to the Australian Bureau of Statistics. According to figures published in 1986, executives and business managers are catching up with farmers — as the hardest workers in terms of hours. Farmers average some 50 hours a week, while executives, administrators and managers average around 48 hours a week. Clerical workers do best in terms of short working hours, at between 36 and 38 hours a week on average while all permanent employees (not casuals) are entitled to four weeks a year holiday on full pay, enhanced by another 17.5 per cent holiday 'loading'.

Wage rates

In 1987, the average male worker in Australia earned around $A450 a week before tax, overtime, or other taxable extras. The average female worker earned about $A90 a week less. At the top end of the scale, according to a survey in 1986, business executives may earn more than $A2,000 a week and the best paid Australians are merchant bankers and advertising executives. Top barristers can earn $A3,000 a day.

For salary earners in non-management positions, the mining industry is relatively well paid, though workers and their families must endure separations or live and work in uncomfortable and isolated circumstances in return for those fat pay packets. Miners and quarrymen averaged some $A603.10 a week in 1986, almost $A100 a week more than the next best-off occupation, those in the 'professional and technical' workers category. The lowest paid were listed as farm workers, averaging $A323.30 a week.

Lurks and perks

Sorry, mates, but since 1986 there have been few company fringe benefits commonly on offer! In 1986 the Federal Government clamped down on this way of boosting a pay packet with attractive 'package deals' like free education for children at choice private schools, company cars and expense accounts. These days all fringe benefits are taxable (see further details in section on taxation). However, some union awards offer subsidised canteen meals, living away from home allowances, superannuation deals, overtime and extra money in return for agreements to use computerised technology or other concessions.

Workers compensation

Workers compensation reimburses employees for injuries or illnesses sustained on the job or otherwise attributed to their jobs or in travelling to and from work. Each State has slightly different laws on the matter though, generally, the claimant does not have to prove his employer was at fault. Nor does it usually matter if the employee was at fault in some way. People qualifying for 'compo' receive a weekly payment to replace their wages, as well as reimbursement for hospital fees, medical expenses or a lump sum payment.

Employers usually refer claims for workers' compensation to their insurance company, which then assesses the case and decides whether to approve payment. If the claim is rejected, the employee can contest the decision through that State or Territory's workers compensation commission or board, and a relevant union may become involved to help.

Superannuation

In the late 1980s, employer-paid superannuation payments became accepted as a bargaining tool, used to persuade unions to moderate inflation-based wage claims. As a result of years of struggle between private employers, the Government and unions, employers in more and more industries agreed to pay a required percentage of each employee's pay packet into a superannuation fund.

The Federal Government and unions have been pushing for a national superannuation scheme. The Government wants to take the pressure off the public purse to pay old age and retirement pensions in future (for more details, see **Australian Health and Welfare**, Chapter 13). At present such pension payments account for a major slice of the Federal Government's massive and ever-growing social security and welfare bill. Independent private and public superannuation schemes already exist for employees of some companies or can be bought into by the self-employed. Tax incentives and investment opportunities are the attractions in running an employee superannuation fund. One of the conflicts in evolving a uniform system of superannuation cover for Australian workers is that trade unions want to administer employers' superannuation contributions on behalf of their members by setting up industry-based funds.

9
Australian Taxation and Company Law

This section aims to show how earning a living in Australia will affect your family, profits, property and business. Taxpayers in Australia pay at three levels, corresponding to the tiers of government: Federal (national), State and local government taxes. Companies and individuals who pay tax can also apply for rebates or exemptions under certain circumstances, at each of the three levels. Most of the tax revenue is paid to the Federal Government which, in turn, redistributes some of this back to the States and, via the States, to local councils.

Tax year

In Australia, the financial year for taxation purposes runs from 1st July to 30th June. The Federal and State budgets — and any changes in taxation — are announced in August. However, 'mini-budgets' at other times in the financial calendar may be used for urgent alterations or to announce new intentions.

PAYE AND PROVISIONAL INCOME TAX

Income tax is levied by the Federal Government via the Australian Tax Office. Under the **Pay As You Earn (PAYE)** system, tax may be deducted directly from pay packets of employees. *Self-employed people must pay 'provisional' income tax* — due in advance on the basis of earnings in the previous year. In these respects, the system of income tax payment and calculation in Australia is similar to that in Britain and many Western countries.

For the self-employed, any shortfall between the provisional tax paid and the tax owed when the year's accounts are finalised must be paid within 30 days of the Australian Tax Office's assessment or on 1st February of the following income tax year, whichever comes first. Provisional tax must be paid quarterly by self-employed people who have paid more than a certain amount of income tax in the previous financial year (at the time of writing, $A2,000 or more). Otherwise, demands for payment of taxes may be adjusted and made payable in twice-yearly instalments, if the taxpayer can convince the Commissioner of Taxation that more than three-quarters of his or her income has been received in the second half of a financial year.

Tax rates

The amount of personal taxation in Australia is comparatively low, according to latest available figures on personal tax rates in OECD countries. Australia ranks in the lower third along with Switzerland, and the USA. The highest rate of personal tax in Australia in 1987 was 49 per cent — though previously people with top incomes paid 55 per cent tax. By comparison, Britain's maximum income tax rate was 60 per cent, and top taxpayers in Japan, France and West Germany paid about 70 per cent, 58 per cent and 56 per cent respectively, though forecasters and governments of these countries predicted a drop in the maximum tax rate to 50 per cent.

But Australians who maintain they are taxed too heavily for the economy's good say that if high personal and indirect taxes don't get 'em — 'bracket creep' will. A 'tax bracket' refers to the level of income on which a particular tax rate is payable (see table opposite). You start paying tax at the lowest rate, and each portion of your income which moves into another bracket attracts a higher rate of tax. The bigger your income, the higher your total tax liability. Australia's level of inflation, at just under 10 per cent annually by the late 1980s, means marked increases in incomes — propelling taxpayers into ever-higher brackets. Regular wage and price increases (indexation) in Australia make 'bracket creep' a plague for its taxpayers; critics of the system point out that you do not need to earn very much for at least part of your income to creep into the top tax bracket. The average wage in Australia is well over $A20,000 a year — and therefore in the 40 per cent bracket. The Business Council of Australia estimated that 48 per cent of Australia's taxpayers faced tax rates of 40 per cent or more in 1987-88. The Federal Government is naturally reluctant to cut its own revenue by indexing tax brackets each year to account for inflation and the upward spiral in people's earnings.

On the opposite page is a guide to the tax rates and income brackets applied in Australia from July 1987, subject to change by successive Federal Governments. Details of current Australian taxes, as they may affect you, can be obtained from Australian high commissions and embassies, State representatives or financial advisers at Australian banks in your country:

Income bracket	Tax rate
$A0-5,100	0 per cent
$A5,101-12,600	24 per cent
$A12,601-19,500	29 per cent
$A19,501-35,000	40 per cent
$A35,000 plus	49 per cent

MEDICARE LEVY

Australian taxpayers are also obliged to pay for the Medicare system of basic public medical and hospital care through a levy on their income, of 1.25 per cent at the time of writing. (For further details on the health care available, see Chapter 13 **Australian Health and Welfare**.)

WHAT INCOME IS TAXABLE?

Residents — be they temporary or permanent, registered for tax as companies, partnerships or individuals — are required to pay tax on income earned in Australia above the minimum tax brackets. Except for some categories of pensioners and low income earners for whom the tax-free level is more generous, beyond the first $A5,100 a year in 1987-88, income is taxable. Income tax is charged on 'assessable income' of an individual. Company tax, at the rate of 49 per cent at time of writing, is levied on companies.

Taxable income includes ordinary trading receipts and investment income as well as salary and wages. 'Gifts' such as lottery wins, legacies, but not including gratuities from an employer to an employee in the course of his or her employment, are outside the income tax assessment. Assessable income may also include:

- profits, after adjustments to account for the impact of inflation, made on sale of 'assets', with some key exceptions, as defined by capital gains tax guidelines given later in this Chapter
- superannuation and retirement lump sum payments, except for money invested in Approved Deposit Funds and Deferred Annuities, and subject to tax concessions in some circumstances (see Chapter 13, **Australian Health and Welfare)**
- allowances, gratuities, compensation, benefits, bonuses, premiums relating to services rendered
- royalities, bounties and subsidies relating to a business, fees or commission for procuring a loan, and certain bonuses relating to life insurance policies
- insurance and indemnity payments for loss of trading stock or loss of profit or income tax that would have been assessable income.

Tax deductions

Some tax deductions can be offset against the liabilities mentioned above. Broadly, the law allows deductions for expenses incurred in gaining or producing. Industrial plant and other commercial equipment owned and used in the process of earning assessable income can normally be written off for tax purposes over three or five years, according to the type of equipment. Taxpayers have the choice of equal annual deductions calculated on the straight line method or claimed on a reducing basis.

In addition to annual deductions, a system of **balancing adjustments** applies when the tax-deductible plant or equipment is sold or destroyed. There is also tax relief available due to destruction, forced disposal or livestock losses due to natural disasters like drought, fire, flood, disease.

There are also tax deductions of up to 150 per cent available as **incentives** to companies and individuals in business to plan and start eligible projects seen as helpful to the Australian economy.

The deductions cover

● basic research
● applied research processes or services

but spending on production or marketing is *not* eligible.

For individual taxpayers who may be paying PAYE, it is possible to reclaim money from the government as rebates for a dependant spouse or housekeeper, for dependant parents or, if the taxpayer is a single parent, for dependant children. Other allowable deductions which may be reclaimed or deducted from tax liabilities include

● trade union or professional dues
● tools of trade
● allowances for certain reading or study materials
● protective clothing

A rebate applies to taxpayers with extremely high medical expenses, (defined as over \$A1,000 at the time of writing) not otherwise covered by the Government's health programmes.

Appeals

All taxpayers have the right to object to assessment made of their tax liabilities by the Australian Taxation Office. An inexpensive system of appeals is provided through the Taxation Boards of Review. As in many countries where tax evasion is a persistent problem, Australia has boosted the staff levels and technology available for investigations of suspected evaders.

COMPANY TAX

For the purposes of the Federal taxation authorities, a 'company' is defined as 'all bodies or associations, corporate or uncorporate', but not including partnerships. There is a flat rate of company tax which, to offset reductions in personal income tax of 1986-87 and the effective abolition of income tax on dividends, was increased from 46 per cent to 49 per cent. Companies cannot claim concessional or zone allowances (which apply only to individuals living in isolated areas) but, subject to certain requirements, may claim deductions for previous years' losses.

Dividends

When company dividends are moved from a parent company to a subsidiary, the **imputation of dividends** provisions (see later in this Chapter) means that, if company tax has already been paid, the subsidiary is not obliged to pay tax again. New laws on imputation of dividends aim to treat companies the same as individual shareholders, in order to encourage investment in Australian resident companies.

Effectively, share dividends (and bonus share issues, which are treated the same way as cash payments) are tax free to the recipient companies (or individuals) — if resident in Australia. If resident overseas, only **dividend withholding tax** (15 per cent at time of writing) applies. Companies issuing dividends must record that company tax has been paid before post-tax dividends are distributed to shareholders or subsidiaries. If not, the bonus shares or dividend payments will be taxed as part of the company's assessable income.

FARMERS, ARTISTS AND ATHLETES

Farmers have special rights to claim deductions for losses incurred in their primary production businesses. And, like artists, authors, performers, inventors and sportsmen and women in Australia, and others accepted as 'abnormal' (irregular) income earners by tax authorities, they are allowed to average their incomes over five years. Tax due is worked out according to a complicated formula, taking into account 'normal' income — from sources like rents, interest, payments from other jobs — which is then added to one-fifth of the taxpayer's 'abnormal' income, as calculated for the five years.

PARTNERSHIPS

In Australia, income tax returns by registered partnerships (see **company law** later in this Chapter) should be lodged whenever two or more people conduct a joint business or joint income-producing activity (but not as a company). The profit or loss is distributed to each partner's taxable income. Partnership agreements are not compulsory but unless there is an agreement stating otherwise, all partners are regarded as having an equal share and will be taxed on this basis.

CAPITAL GAINS TAX

After much controversy over whether a Labor Party Government would ever do it, the Federal government introduced a capital gains tax. It is said that Australia's middle classes don't like the capital gains tax any more than the mega-rich, at whom it was ostensibly aimed, since the tax extends to some of their previously tax-exempt investments, too. Since it was announced late in 1985, there has been some sorting out and addition to the fine print to determine exactly which profits and payments are taxable under its regulations. Broadly, Australia's capital gains tax:

- is levied at the taxpayer's ordinary rate of personal or company taxation, after the increase in the 'retail price index' (an inflation indicator) has been subtracted from the initial profit along with its original cost to the owner, to calculate the gain on the investment, in real terms
- is applied to realised (sold) assets bought after 19th September 1985
- allows realised nominal losses to be offset against it
- treats as 'realisation' the disposal of assets as 'gifts', with the recipient being taxed on a gift received on its fair market value.

Importantly, this tax will *not* apply to inheritances arising from the death of an asset-holder. Broadly, there are **no death duties applicable in Australia**. Capital gains tax will only be levied if the assets are actually sold by an administrator of a deceased estate or disposed of for money by a beneficiary. Exemptions from the capital gains tax include:

- the taxpayer's principal residence and a 'reasonable' tract of land around it. However, no exemption applies on houses owned by a family trust or private company and lived in by a trust beneficiary or shareholder
- superannuation or life insurance policies
- sale of motor vehicles and other personal-use assets (like furniture) with a disposable value below a certain amount (under $A5,000 at time of writing)

Nor does the tax apply to 'rollovers' (ie arrangements to reinvest and so defer a capital gains tax liability), compensation payments for stolen or destroyed property, and asset ownership changes associated with certain types of business reorganisations. Expenditures in buying, improving or selling an asset are all part of the capital gains tax assessment of the value of the property, and the amount of profit made in selling it. However, as a general rule, annual expenses such as repairs and interest payments on the asset, whether for business or non-business purposes, will be excluded from the asset cost base and calculation of any tax owing.

FRINGE BENEFITS TAX

Fringe benefits may still be part of a job package for, say, a temporary employee 'imported' from overseas who may have certain tax-exempt extras built into his payments for work while in Australia. Foreign consultants, for example, may still have relocation expenses, occupational health and counselling, safety and long service awards, holiday travel and children's education built in to their job offer in Australia, because these are still free of tax to the company.

But, generally, the inclusion of non-cash benefits like these which people are offered as part of a job package in Australia has dropped dramatically. This is because the Federal Government's series of tax reforms in the mid 1980s (including the capital gains tax described above) reduced opportunities for companies and employees to minimise their tax burden through 'fringe benefits'. Apart from axing the 'business lunch' and entertainment costs undertaken 'on the company' and previously deducted from taxable income, the government imposed the 'fringe benefits tax'. Like capital gains, its new and largely unpopular nature meant a number of fine tunings to make it both more equitable and efficient. Since July 1986 all fringe benefits have been considered part of a person's or company's taxable income.

Fringe benefits tax rates
All fringe benefits to employees (or the self-employed) are taxable at the company rate (49 cents in the dollar, at time of writing). An employer's tax liability in this area includes

- company cars
- free or low-interest loans
- free or subsidised accommodation or board
- goods and services sold at a reduced rate or provided free (above a certain amount, in the case of employees)
- expenses paid on behalf of an employee

Staff canteens and employer-provided superannuation schemes as well as employee share acquisition schemes are exempt. The tax on company cars was set at 24 per cent unless substantial long-distance use of the vehicle is proved, in which case the tax is lower.

Exemptions and concessions
Board and accommodation provided for live-in help to care for a disabled or disadvantaged person are among the exemptions, while rental housing and other benefits like holiday travel provided to workers in remote areas are only taxable above 50 per cent of their value.

LIVING AWAY FROM HOME ALLOWANCES

Employers are taxed the company rate if they pay employees a living away from home subsidy. However, 'reasonable' costs for food and accommodation are not subject to the fringe benefit tax.

ENTERTAINMENT

No deductions are allowed for expenses such as business meals, drinks, cocktail parties, tickets and so forth, whether undertaken in Australia or overseas — for local or foreign customers. If your business does extensive promotions overseas, it is best to apply for a grant or exemption under the variety of Government incentives to trade and industry.

BANK ACCOUNT DEBIT TAX

Known as the BAD, this tax is on cheque accounts on debits: 10 cents (at latest rates) on $A100 or less, progressively increasing to a maximum of $A1 on debits of $A5,000 or more.

SALES TAX, EXCISE AND IMPORT DUTY

In Australia there is no Value Added Tax (VAT) or equivalent penalty on consumers, though it is proposed from time to time by advocates of indirect taxation. Instead, there is a sales tax on goods, whether made in Australia or not. Different sales tax percentages and 'schedules' apply to a wide variety of consumer goods and services. The policy is to hit luxuries rather than necessities. Thus the prices of imported cars, swimming pool equipment, licensed computer software, films and video recordings have risen in recent years. Though they often aim to cut income taxes on one hand, Federal governments regularly extend consumption taxes to items previously exempt — recent examples (1986-87 budget) being bathroom fittings, hot air balloons and gliders.

Alcohol, cigarettes and petrol tend to be regular casualties of the Federal budget in August.

IMPUTATION OF COMPANY DIVIDENDS

This system is a tax incentive to encourage people or companies to invest in stocks and shares of resident companies, by making share dividends effectively tax free in Australia. If a company pays the necessary company tax (49 per cent) on its profits before distributing its dividends or bonus share issues, the shareholders will *not* be taxed on this part of their income. Furthermore, shareholders in a lower tax bracket (paying less than the 49 per cent company rate), will receive a tax credit for the tax already paid by the company on that dividend.

The tax removed before the dividend is distributed to a shareholder is credited to the shareholder's income tax assessment as tax already paid. So, for each $A51 of eligible dividends received (based on the company already paying tax at 49 per cent), the individual is assessed for $A100, on which $A49 has already been paid in tax. With imputation, the shareholder's income from dividends is tax free. This incentive applies to non-residents (who only pay dividend withholding tax at 15 per cent if the company tax was not paid before the dividend was issued) as well as to resident investors in Australian-based companies. However, if the company cannot show it has already paid due tax on the dividend, tax is payable at the recipient's usual rate.

INTERNATIONAL DOUBLE TAXATION AGREEMENTS

People from, or with investments in, countries sharing a double taxation agreement with Australia may find themselves off the hook in some aspects of their obligation to pay tax on their various incomes. However, if your country of origin has no such agreement on taxation with Australia it is best before you leave to consult experts on both Australia and your own country to discover how much money you may be required to pay while earning in Australia, and on returning home. Extra tax liabilities may also arise when you try to move your money from one country to another, especially if a tax haven is involved.

Australia has *comprehensive double taxation agreements* with Britain, the USA, Canada, New Zealand, Singapore, Japan, France, Belgium, the Netherlands, Malaysia, Korea, Ireland, Norway, Italy, Denmark and Sweden, as well as *limited agreements* with India and Greece.

These agreements usually mean that the country where people have been contracted to work temporarily has a primary right to tax their income. The other contracting country, the worker's country of residence, also has the right to claim taxes due but, if it does so, it must allow credit for the amount already paid where the income originated. For example, you may be undertaking a temporary job in Australia paid at a rate which puts you in the 40 per cent tax bracket for Australia. In the meantime, you would normally be paying income tax at a 50 per cent rate for that amount in your country of residence. So the first 40 per cent of income tax will be levied by Australia, and the other 10 per cent by the country where you normally live.

Exceptions
However, in some cases the agreement may provide a reduction or even an exemption from tax imposed by the country where the income originated. For instance, Australia does not levy a tax on non-residents' income from dividends and shareholdings in Australian companies if company tax has already been paid (See **Company Tax** and **Imputation of Company Dividends** above).

Royalties
Agreements with Britain, the USA, Canada, Korea, Singapore, France, the Federal Republic of Germany, the Netherlands, Switzerland, Belgium, Sweden, Denmark, Norway, Ireland and Italy mean that the Australian tax on most royalties derived by the residents of those countries may not exceed 10 to 15 per cent of the royalties. But this limitation does not apply if the royalties are effectively connected with the permanent establishment of the recipient in Australia.

Royalties included in this provision are

● industrial and copyright royalties
● payment for use of equipment
● know-how payments

Exceptions are mining and other natural resource royalties and royalties derived from 'permanent establishment of' the beneficial owner in the country in which they originate. If the country of residence also taxes royalties, the tax authorities party to the agreement on royalties will allow a credit for tax paid in the other country.

Pensions and annuities
Pensions and personal annuities are exempt from taxation in the country of source, whether or not they are taxable in the country of residence. As is commonly the case in Australia's double-taxation agreements, payments by British-based employers to employees working in Australia, but resident in Britain, are subject to British — *not* Australian — taxes in the following circumstances:

- if the time spent in Australia is not more than 183 days in the income year and/or
- if such paid work is *not* done as part of the process of 'permanent establishment' in Australia

An intending migrant laying the groundwork for living and working in Australia permanently would be subject to Australian taxation.

If the working visit by a British resident is longer than 183 days, the fees or wages paid are subject to Australian tax though a credit will be given against tax owed in Britain. If the services are performed in Australia at a 'fixed base' readily available to a British resident, tax would be levied in Australia on the same basis as for trading profits. It is up to the employer to decide: he can forego any deduction from his own taxable income for the wages he pays the British resident, or he can claim a deduction but leave the employee liable to pay Australian tax. The tax rate which applies depends on whether the earner has incorporated his talents, and so pays at company rates, or if he remains a personal tax payer subject to income tax brackets.

THE AUSTRALIA CARD

There has been such staunch opposition in so many quarters to the idea of printed personal identification, known as the Australia Card, that the enabling legislation has been held up in the Federal parliament. However, the Labor adminstration in Canberra has repeatedly said that it plans to introduce the card; if it succeeds in passing the new law, the Australia Card should be a reality by 1988. The Federal Government is keen on the Australia Card concept in order to stamp out tax evasion and social security fraud. It also expects to make it harder for illegal immigrants and people who have overstayed their visas in Australia to gain paid employment and/or take advantage of social services without being identified.

The proposed Australia Card would make it necessary for newcomers to the country to register and be issued with a card in order to identify them for social security benefits and public health care under the Medicare system. The card would be necessary for key financial transactions — like opening a bank account as well as for presentation to new employers to register for payment of income tax. Children would be registered on their parents' cards.

STATE GOVERNMENT TAXES

Payroll tax is the biggest source of tax revenue for Australian State and Territory governments. Employers are generally required to lodge monthly returns, and the rate is about 5 per cent in most places. Small businesses with only a few people on their payrolls may be exempt from payroll tax, and the need to send returns to the State Department of Taxation. All States have abolished death or estate duties.

Stamp Duty

Stamp duty, however, is payable to State taxation authorities on a range of documents and transactions. These include

- transfers of marketable securities
- cheques and bills of exchange
- registrations and transfers of motor vehicles and trailers
- partnership deeds
- powers and letters of attorney
- company documents (in New South Wales)
- declarations of trusts
- instalment purchase agreements

Rates vary according to the transaction's value or, in other cases, are set at a fixed rate.

Land Tax

Land tax is also imposed by all States and Territories of Australia on the value of land at differing rates, depending on the tax law in that State. But land used for certain types of primary production or farming, and residential land which is the site of the owners home, are exempt partly or in full, depending on the State or Territory involved.

Financial Institutions Duty

Financial institutions duty is levied in New South Wales, Victoria, South Australia and Western Australia on all credits or accounts conducted with financial institutions — a charge which may be passed onto their clients. At the time of writing, the rate was 3 cents per $A100 with a maximum of $A300 payable on any individual deposit of $A1m or more.

Motorists

Driver licence and car registration fees are also the tax prerogative of Australia's States and Territories. These vary and are charged on an annual, renewable basis (see Chapter 11, **Driving in Australia**).

LOCAL GOVERNMENT TAXES

Local governments comprise city councils, boroughs, shires and municipalities. They levy taxes on land value of private property or on its 'annual' value, on both houses and businesses. Called **rates**, this money is used by the locality for building control, health inspection facilities and garbage collection and disposal (though in some places garbage services are covered by a separate levy). Roads, footpaths, town planning, parks and recreational facilities, public libraries as well as community and welfare services, are also supported by ratepayers' monies and administered by the elected local council.

ESTABLISHING A BUSINESS — COMPANY LAW

Australia has a uniform scheme of company regulations operating in all six States and two Territories, subject to some minor local modifications. There are four Federal Acts plus a number of State legal Codes which apply. State **corporate affairs commissions** bear the brunt of making sure that everyday details in overseeing companies comply with the regulations, though at higher levels both State and Federal attorney-generals' departments are responsible. The overall scheme of company regulations is administered by the **National Companies and Securities Commission** (NCSC).

Business types
There are a variety of ways to conduct your business in Australia:

- by an individual operating as a **sole trader** — either as a principal or representative, with sole liability for debts incurred
- two or more people, though generally no more than 20, forming a **partnership** in which each partner is liable for debts incurred
- **companies** may be formed by five people or more or, in the case of **proprietary companies**, by two or more people. The liability of the company is usually limited and the profits distributed in the form of dividends. People forming a company must subscribe their names to a **memorandum of association** and comply with State laws.It may be limited by share or guarantee as an unlimited company, or in the case of mining, as a no-liability company.

Registration
Whether starting up a new company in Australia or establishing either a branch or subsidiary of a foreign-based company, the necessary documents have to be registered and lodged with a State or Territory Government. This allows your business to be conducted throughout the country. Whether a foreign-based business sets up as a branch or incorporates as an Australia subsidiary is up to that company, but consulting with Australian tax experts may reveal clear advantages either way, depending on the latest changes or interpretation of tax laws.

10
Housing and Property

Australians live and work in some strange sounding places. Don't laugh! — you, too, could end up in Winji Jimmi, Kangy Angy, Tom Ugly's Point or Wobby Beach.

However, supressing a giggle at Aussie place names will be the least of your problems on arrival in Australia. Never mind what it's called — where and how do you start looking for a home? What about a commercial property? Should you be thinking about buying or renting?

Buying and renting

As a rule, it is best to buy rather than rent, since rents are high in most of the bigger urban centres. But house and flat prices around Australia have suddenly boomed, especially in the choicest commercial and domestic locations.

The language of real estate is a whole new aspect of Ausslang, so the addition of a few common terms and abbreviations in this section will help as you squint through columns of fine printed property advertisements in the local newspapers. Familiarise yourself with the latest prices by scanning available newspapers at the nearest Australian embassy or high commission. Some State Governments also keep would-be residents up to date by distributing the latest real estate listings.

SOMEWHERE TO LIVE

Housing is one of the most vexing questions facing anybody moving to a new country and one that should be considered well in advance of the event. Unless you are a student with plans to live in a university or college, or are staying with friends or relatives, at least at first, be sure your expectations and arrangements for a place to live are well made and realistic. Even if a contact or employer has made and confirmed an offer to supply housing on arrival, you may soon want to enter the real estate market independently as a buyer/investor. However, most people decide to rent first, while getting to know the area as well as jobs, schools and social life and discovering whether Australia is for them longer term.

RENTING A PROPERTY

Below is a survey of weekly rent most people paid (the median) for a two-bedroom flat or home unit in Australian capital cities in November 1986. Bear in mind that by 1987 rents had increased by at least the rate of inflation (about 8%).

Sydney	Melbourne	Brisbane	Adelaide	Perth	Canberra
$A104.87	$A95.51	$A80.65	$A88.51	$A94.98	$A130.29

(Figures provided by the Real Estate Institute of Australia)

Rents are considerably cheaper outside the big cities. In the late 1980s rent prices around Australia rose steadily due to the drying up of investment in housing. Previously there was a taxation incentive to people who let blocks of units or houses for amounts less than their mortgage repayments on the property. Such investors are no longer permitted to offset this shortfall against other income, and that's one reason why rents rose and the property market for domestic letting shrank.

As for commercial property, a prime location in Sydney or Melbourne is more expensive than any other city. The space in large commercial buildings and complexes is let by the square metre and, like the domestic rental sector, finding a vacancy can be a competitive business.

Below is a guide to office and industrial rents in Australian capital cities in December 1986 provided by a major real estate company:

Rents in Australian dollars per square metre		
	Prime Office	Prime Industrial
Sydney	540	94
Melbourne	410	70
Adelaide	185	55
Brisbane	330	70
Perth	260	50
Canberra	245	55

The other tax-related reason for a tight rental market was the introduction of a capital gains tax (see Chapter 9). This is levied at the person or company's standard tax rate on sale of an **investment property** other than the house or unit which is the owner's actual residence; only *one* such home is allowed per owner. **Rent control** is *not* widespread in Australia, and has been abolished entirely in Tasmania and Western Australia. In other States control over residential rents does not apply to new premises or tenancies after a certain date. It is illegal for property owners to discriminate against a would-be tenant on the grounds of sex or marital status or because they are pregnant, under the Federal Government's Sexual Discrimination Act.

Housing options

For the desperate newcomer who has not made adequate housing arrangements in advance, accommodation may be available at a **Commonwealth migrant hostel** — though these are not the most heartening places in which to start life in a new country. If you're financially stretched, **council housing** may also be available though in many places the waiting lists are long. Families with young children, the elderly or people otherwise in greatest financial or medical need are favoured. The standard of council accommodation is often far below that of the private sector and may comprise soulless estates and tacky highrise tenements. Yet there are some excellent, award-winning examples of domestic architecture in the public sector: attractive, compact units in well landscaped settings.

Finding accommodation

The best places to start, if you plan to rent a house or business property in Australia, are local newspapers and real estate agents. Such agents often specialise in property management. In the housing market, short leases are sometimes available; a private agreement may mean that after it has expired the owner will allow you to stay on a weekly or monthly basis. But usually a first lease is set at 6 months and extendable depending on whether you and the owner come to agreement on rent increases. Properties are let either furnished or unfurnished, the former usually more expensive. When renting somewhere to live, the lease is normally clear enough for the layman to understand and paying for legal advice is usually unnecessary.

However, if renting a **commercial property** it is best to take the advice of a solicitor. Commercial leases are more complex and may be negotiated at a set rental for generally longer periods. Such a lease may be 'sold' to a new tenant approved by the property owner (and the local zoning authorities, depending on the type of business and if it is to change) when a current tenant plans to move before it expires.

In addition to real estate agents and newspapers, State and Territory Governments often keep **registers** of serviced industrial land while, at local government level, **zoning restrictions** may stand in the way of using a property for a particular business or industrial purpose; it is always best to check with these authorities for information and advice about your proposed rental.

The payment of **rates** is not usually an additional expense for the tenant, since this should be accounted for by the landlord. However, tenants are responsible for paying electricity, telephone, gas and similar connection and upkeep charges. An **inventory** of items in the property — especially if a furnished house or flat — is usually drawn up along with the lease. It is advisable to study this list of furniture and fittings carefully before you sign, to make sure it is accurate.

Bonds

Renting a home in Australia will normally involve the payment of a bond as well as rent. This often amounts to four to six weeks' rental, as well as a month or so of rent in advance. This could add up to hundreds, even thousands, of dollars — so be prepared. Failure to vacate the premises leaving furniture and fittings behind and in reasonable condition (meaning 'reasonable' wear and tear) may mean that the landlord can draw on the bond you lodged on taking the lease, to pay for replacements and repairs. Similarly, all or part of the bond may be forfeited if the tenant defaults on payment or conditions of the lease.

BUYING PROPERTY

Home ownership rates in Australia are probably the highest in the world. Around 70 per cent of the population owns or is in the process of buying a place to live. Buying a home in Australia is a fine investment, as most properties hold their own against inflation as time goes on. The owner may count on a profit of a few per cent more than if they kept the same initial investment in a bank for a few years.

People wanting to immigrate are generally expected to show their commitment to their new country, if they can afford it, and buy a place to live. If coming from a country with a good exchange rate in comparison to the Australian dollar — ie most developed countries, during the late 1980s due to the weakness in the Australian currency — purchasing a home in Australia is one of the most attractive prospects of the move. However, if you must borrow money to buy a home, it is not easy to raise a full **mortgage** and/or claim a tax concession, unless you are a low income earner and therefore eligible for government assistance.

Below are the prices paid most often (the median) for 'established houses' in each of the capital cities of Australia in 1985-86. However, by 1987 prices in many places had almost doubled.

Sydney	Melbourne	Brisbane	Adelaide	Perth	Canberra
$A98,000	$A82,900	$A61,300	$A77,100	$A53,900	$A92,300

(Figures provided by the Real Estate Institute of Australia)

An **established** property refers to a house which is already completed and previously inhabited. Otherwise, Australians commonly buy **project** or **estate** homes from plans for new suburban developments. In inner city areas, terraces or townhouses comprising one or more stories and attached to other such buildings are common, as are **home units**, otherwise known as apartments or flats.

Undercover parking or garage areas are an important feature in Australia's sprawling suburban streetscapes. On the coast, the opportunity to take your car off the road and under cover is particularly important because of the sea air, and the hazard of salt rusting the metal. The same applies to external metallic features of a house or flat. These also degenerate quickly in the sea air and ugly rusty smears or flaking paintwork from metal window frames and balcony railings are a common sight in many seaside suburbs.

'Average' homes — established or brand new, whether houses or flats — will have two or three bedrooms, more than one bathroom, a laundry and plenty of outdoor living area, for land is usually cheap and plentiful. Detached homes commonly occupy no more than half the site. 'Room for a pool' is common in Australian real estate jargon; it means you can expect a big garden with lots of space for outdoor entertaining. Electricity, and natural gas provide most lighting, heating and other power needs. Where land is scarcer, as in central metropolitan areas, high rise flats and townhouses — often most elegant and attractive — can offer marvellous views; they usually feature at least one large balcony, as well as external courtyards and off-street, two-car parking facilities. The plusher home unit developments include outdoor swimming pools, tennis courts and even sauna baths, since Australians are keen on having their luxuries at home, even if they have to share them.

However, if buying in a more isolated or new suburban location, don't take it for granted that drainage and sewerage (or even electricity and telephone cables) will be installed. Septic sewerage, rain water tanks, on-site eletricity generators and dirt roads are what you can expect if 'going

bush' — otherwise known as getting away from city living to occupy a
farm or other secluded site.

FORMS OF ENTITLEMENT

There are a variety of forms of ownership applicable to property in
Australia:

Freehold Estate (fee simple)
This is the most common and desirable estate entitlement. It means the
owner has exclusive right to the use of the property and no one but the
Crown (Federal Government) can interfere with that right. The
Government may be able to serve an acquisition order to buy up all or
part of the property for, say, road works. There could be other
complications you should enquire about, too, if considering a freehold,
like an easement to the State sewerage and water supply authority
(meaning it has the right to lay pipes on that land).

Leasehold Estate
This is the next best thing to a freehold. A person may lease property
from a Government or from a private owner of a freehold estate. For
instance, in the Australian Capital Territory it is generally not possible to
buy a freehold, and 99-year Crown leases are the norm for home owners.
Other forms of leasehold may be a life entitlement which may be
specified in a will referring to a deceased's property.

Documents of Title
In the case of freehold ownership, one of two documents may be issued
by the Government — **Certificate of Title** or **Strata Title.**
   Certificate of Title is usually issued by the State or Territory's **Lands
Title Office.** It keeps a record of who owns each particular piece of land,
and the relevant document is called Certificate of Title. The Government
keeps the original while the owner is given a copy. This copy, along with
mortgage documents if a loan has been taken to buy the property, is
usually filed at the Land Title Office. Each successive owner of the piece
of land is mentioned on the Certificate of Title. If the owner decides to
lease the land, this transaction must appear on the certificate. If the land
is sold, the certificate becomes the property of the new owner. Freehold
title, as proved by the Certificate of Title, means that the current owner
has rights over the land and whatever is above it — literally, from the
centre of the earth to the sky. However, mineral rights to such a property
are reserved by the Crown.
   Strata Title is a document showing ownership of part of an allotment

of land or for a 'piece of air' (stratum). It normally applies to home units and shows the owner has a share in the land surface and whatever lies above it. Each owner of a unit, flat or apartment on the land block has a copy of the Strata Title. Maintainance of common areas, like driveways and gardens, is the responsibility of all title holders for that property and subject to 'fair and reasonable' rules. Strata Title holders must agree to these rules, which are enforceable.

Company Title

This is the old-fashioned and increasingly rare entitlement to property on which flats have been built — the predecessor to the Strata Title. It is sometimes more difficult to raise a bank or building society mortgage on this type of ownership, due to its great complexity. Broadly, Company Title means that the right to occupy part of a property is via shares issued by a company which owns the property. The buyer acquires shares in the company.

OBTAINING A HOME LOAN

Savings banks and building societies provide most of the finance for housing in Australia, through partial mortgages on the purchase price. Prospective owners must raise the rest of the money, known as their 'deposit', themselves. The necessary deposit is around 25 per cent of the total amount, but personal equity amounting to about 15 per cent of the price may be acceptable to some lending institutions. Although it is sometimes possible to raise this extra money through a finance company or 'second mortgage,' banks and building societies will usually refuse to fund the deal if they know about it or have not approved this themselves. The lending policies of most banks and building societies provide loans for the building of new houses or established properties.

There is no fixed loan limit, though they do not normally exceed 75 per cent of the financial institution's valuation of the property. However, in special cases and subject to a maximum of $A40,000 (at the time of writing) and with mortgage loan insurance (at extra cost to the buyer), it may be possible to extend the mortgage to 95 per cent of the property's value. The size of the loan is based on the amount of repayments the purchaser can afford. This is calculated as no more than 30 per cent of his or her post-tax monthly income. The buyer must provide proof that he or she has the stated income. At the time of writing, there were no tax concessions like interest rate rebates applicable to first home buyers in Australia, though these have been available in the past. Interest rates of about 15.5 per cent were typical in 1987. The terms of home loans range from 15 to 25 years, or before the buyer's retirement age (65 years for a man, 60 for a woman).

Banks tend to be more choosy than building societies about offering home loans; they can afford to be, since their interest rates are lower than those of building societies. Banks usually require applicants to have a history of saving with them of at least 12 months.

Stamp duty is levied by State and Territory Governments on all real estate transactions, though in the case of first home buyers, different governments may waive all or part of the duty.

Apart from banks and building societies, Federal, State and Territory housing authorities may provide finance, often through insurance or superannuation organisations. Life assurance companies, mortgage brokers, credit unions, solicitors funds and finance companies may also be helpful in raising the money you need to buy a home or another property.

AUSSIE REAL ESTATE JARGON

*Prop. cl. Dandenong sol 2b'rm det. cnr bv. Lge ver.,wiwo cpbds, all elfs., f/covs., ven blds incl...*what is it all about? Who would ever guess that the above is an advertisement offering a property for sale which, according to the vendors, is close to Dandenong (outside Melbourne, in Victoria), solid, two-bedroomed, detached, on a corner, and built of brick veneer? Or that it features a large verandah and walk-in-walk-out cupboards? Included in the price are all electric light fittings, floor coverings and venetian blinds.

Australian real estate advertisements are often couched in a special jargon which can be frustrating even for Aussies — so how is a new resident to cope? For the uniquely Australian style of housing has developed to cater for climates ranging from tropical to desert dry, then perhaps freezing in winter. The resulting architectural and interior fittings and features may surprise you.

The brief Real Estate Dictionary which follows may be useful when you start scanning newspaper advertisements and agency brochures in quest of a property to buy or rent. As you'll see, in Australia they call a sitting or drawing room a 'lounge', the wc a 'toilet', and interior cupboards any number of things.

The key words in Aussie property dealings — whether commercial premises or a home to live in is what you have in mind — reflect the expectations of the market. This list indicates the kind of heating, floor covering, cooking, laundry and other arrangements ordinary people expect to find in a property.

An Aussie Real Estate Dictionary

alc	alcove	estab	established
awso	all weather sleep out	exh fan	exhaust fan
appr	approximately	ext	external
avail	available		
Av	avenue	feat	feature
		fitts	fittings
bal/blce	balcony	flr	floor
bsn	basin	fluor lts	fluorescent lights
bath/bathrm	bathroom	f/wire doors	fly wire doors
bh	bath heater	f/wire scrns	fly wire screens
b'fast	breakfast	Fwy	freeway
bib	built-in bath	fr drs	french doors
bics	built-in cupboards	frt	front
bir	built-in wardrobe	f/furn	fully furnished
br	brick	f/tld	fully tiled
bus	business		
bv	brick veneer	g.i.	galvanised iron
		grdn	garden
crpt	carpet	grge	garage
crpt sq	carpet square	gbh	gas bath heater
ct	cement tiles	g cpr	gas copper
ctr	cement trough	g htr	gas heater
cnr	corner	ghws	gas hot water service
conc	concrete	g spc htr	gas space heater
covs	coverings	gds	glass doors
crt	court	govt	government
Crs	Crescent	Gve	Grove
crtns	curtains		
		htr	heater
dep	deposit	htg	heating
det	detached	holl blds	holland blinds
d'ette	dinette	hs	high school
dng rm	dining room		
dbl/dble	double	incl	including
dbss	double bowl stainless steel sink	ins	insurance
		int	interest
df	double fronted		
dt	dressing table	kit	kitchen
Dr	Drive	k'ette	kitchenette
E	east		
elect	electric	lam	laminex
elHWS/ehws	electric hot water system	lge	large
		lp	linen press
elfs	electric light fittings	LA	Listing Agent
elev	elevated	lu	lock up (as in lu grge)
encl	enclosed	lnge	lounge (ie sitting room)

mins	minutes	sf	single fronted
mod	modern	sh	sink heater
mort	mortgage	so	sleep out (enclosed verandah)
mos	mosaic	sol	solid
mth	months	sav	stock at valuation
		sss	stainless steel sink
N	north	sstr	stainless steel trough
ncs	nearest cross street	stv	stove
		St	Street
o/o	owner occupied		
ofp	open fire place	tce/trace	terrace
ono	or nearest offer	timb	timbered
op	off peak (as in hot water)	tld	tiled
opport	opportunity	trzo	terrazo
opp	opposite	tct	terra cotta tiles
		thru	through
Pde	Parade	t'out/thru'out	throughout
parq	parquetry	toil	toilet
ped bsn	pedestal basin	tbir	triple built-in wardrobe
p a	per annum		
p m	per month	ven blds	venetian blinds
p w	per week	ver	verandah
Pl	Place	v/fl	vinyl floor
pol flr	polished floor	v/tls	vinyl tiles
prop	property	vol	volume
purch	purchaser		
		W	west
qual	quality	wb	weather board
		wir	walk in wardrobe
rec	recess	wiwo	walk-in-walk-out
ref	references	wipantry	walk-in pantry
req	required	w/minster	westminster (a carpet-style floor covering)
rend	rendered		
rd	road	w/w	wall to wall
rm	room	wk	week
rch	rotary clothes hoist	w/ends	weekends
rotis	rotisserie	w/m	washing machine
rc	rough cast	w/shed	woodshed
		w/shop	workshop
S	south	w i	wrought iron
sep	separate		
shwr rec	shower recess	yr	year
sgle	single		

11
Driving in Australia

Pleasures, problems and the police

Wide open spaces can make Australia a fine place to drive — but no place for wimps on wheels. In remote regions, as well as the cities and towns, long distances between destinations are to be expected. It's nothing for an Australian to drive for an hour to two simply to call on people or find a picnic ground. Sensibly, major transport routes are designed to include rest areas, speed ramps and other conveniences for cars and drivers obliged to cover long distances, rather than for considerations of pedestrians, kangaroos or koalas crossing (of which more later).

But don't expect always perfect planning. In bigger centres or at key crossroads, traffic snarls, bottlenecks and problems are the norm. Regional governments, responsible for maintaining and planning roads, are often tardy in committing vast sums needed to improve traffic links and wait for the Federal Government to step in with finance. Sydney, for example, has lived for decades with hellish peak hour jams on its famous coathanger Harbour Bridge, as too many cars try to cross this crucial but narrow artery at the same time. Baking inside the car as you try to crawl a few blocks is an irritating fact of city life in a land of hot and humid summers, encouraging a nation of often brash and 'stroppy' (bad tempered) motorists.

Dawdling in order to gawp at the scenery on both 'primary' and 'secondary' routes can be dangerous. Driving hundreds or thousands of kilometres — often through the night — an eagerness to arrive at long last, plus the unchanging scenery and straight roads that seem to go on for ever, may also impair ability to see other vehicles and judge their speed. The standard of Australia's 16,000 km national highway system linking major towns and cities is high, but isolation, perpetual roadworks, bushfires, floods or droughts often make Australia's sealed roads inaccessible. Minor routes are another matter. Sometimes no more than rock and gravel, they can be a hazard of driving life in Australia.

130

Even Australia's north-south link, the 3,000 km Stuart Highway from Adelaide in South Australia to Darwin in the Northern Territory, was at last sealed with bitumen and suitable for heavy traffic as late as 1987. After bumping along a dirt track for a few hours, it is little wonder that nuts and bolts holding together the occupants — as well as the vehicle — break or come loose. Driving unsealed roads requires skill, patience and preparation in case you are stranded in the middle of nowhere with a cracked axle or universal joint,waiting for the next driver to come along.

Main city and tourist routes feature six to eight lane **expressways** — the Australian term for super-highways known as motorways in Britain, autoroutes, autobahns and autostradas in continental Europe and freeways in the United States. Occasionally, **tolls** are levied to help cover the expensive business of highway building and maintenance in a vast continent. Lighting is sophisticated on major arteries and usually good elsewhere.

Koalas crossing

Most roads are well signposted to warn of unexpected bends and treacherous conditions or flooding. Uniquely Aussie wildlife signs are a feature of driving in the bush or outback and even in semi-urban areas. These signs may seem a joke, with their warnings of 'Kangaroos 5km' or 'Koalas Crossing' above silhouettes of the beasts. However, they are not there merely to protect the wildlife from vehicles. Large animals like kangaroos or wallabies moving at speed across or along a road present a real danger to cars and their occupants, and can cause accidents when emerging suddenly from the scrub, taking a driver by surprise. Vehicles in rural areas are often fitted with large 'roo bars in case they strike an animal, to minimise damage to the car or truck and provide some psychological protection to the person behind the wheel. An unprotected car colliding with a kangaroo or wild pig at high speed is unlikely to escape unscathed.

Air conditioning is a 'must' for serious driving in Australia. It enhances the ability to sit out a traffic jam or drive long distances in searing temperatures. Whether you are planning to buy a car in Australia or take one with you on moving there, have your vehicle fitted with a decent air conditioner or at least a strong fan. Just as most of us wouldn't dream of driving without good interior heating and windscreen demisters in the colder climes of the northern hemisphere, air conditioning is virtually standard for the family car Down Under.

Be prepared

Given the long distances and — in comparison to Britain or Western

Europe — a relatively sparse road network, not to mention the temptations to see the bush, desert or rural landscape by literally getting off the beaten track, it's advisable to carry extra water and fuel for your car on long journeys. Many outdoorsy types with extra boot space stick to the 'have barbie — will travel' principle, they always carry a portable barbecue and bag of charcoal...just in case they run into that extra-special spot for a swim and some food in an idyllic beach or bushland setting, or if they are too weary to drive on. But you don't need expensive equipment — a 'billy' (metal pot with a wire handle) and some kind of improvised grilling rack will do the job, and is what most rural Australians use.

But be certain you don't light a campfire in a **bushfire zone**, or when a warning has been issued. And the golden rule is never, never leave until every last spark has been extinguished, preferably by covering the embers with dirt or sand. The danger of starting a bushfire is ever present in the Australian bush. For the same reason, never throw your cigarette butts or matches out of the car window — it's the easiest way to start a fire which could cause serious loss of life and property.

ROAD RULES

Don't commence your driving career in Australia with abuse from fellow road users, unwelcome encounters with those persons in blue (police), parking fines...or worse. Familiarise yourself with the driving rules and signposting which apply. Bear in mind that while the general laws of motoring around Australia are fairly uniform, and similar to those of most Western societies, some aspects could be totally alien to first time drivers there.

Just as driving conditions alter around the country, so do the rules applying in the States and Territories of Australia. Each is responsible for writing and administering its own road laws, and the police forces co-operate to exchange data about criminal and traffic offences across borders. Stiff fines, jail terms and licence suspension are among the penalties for drink-driving convictions (see section below). For other more minor driving offences like speeding, most States use a **points system**. A driver's points are deducted according to the magnitude of each traffic offence. If all points are lost by an individual within a certain time period, the licence is withdrawn as punishment.

The changes in road rules between States are often small, though on matters like priority at intersections the variation can be dangerous, so it is a good idea to obtain the *Highway Codebook* for both the region you are to live in and elsewhere, if you plan an interstate drive. Basically, all States adhere to the 'keep to the left' principle, the driver sitting to the right of the passenger as in Britain. The wearing of **seat belts** is compulsory. Picking up hitch hikers is not recommended in most places — and is illegal in Victoria. As detailed a little later in this Chapter, different States and Territories vary in their requirements for drivers from overseas who may be allowed to use foreign licences in Australia. These rules are a key consideration if your job or circumstances mean you depend on driving for a living.

SPEED LIMITS

Since the roads and conditions tend to be fine and clear, many people feel an urge to break the speed limit and test themselves and their vehicles. The temptation to live out your Grand Prix fantasies on the spectacular S-bends of Sydney's eastern suburbs and go zooming down to the harbour is hard for many to resist. However, traffic policing is tough and the road toll remains unacceptably high in most places. Those who speed habitually run a high risk of that cop car looming in the rear vision mirror before they can say 'New Australian'.

Speeds are measured in kilometres, and cars are usually required to have speedometres which provide a reading in these terms. In built-up areas — defined as those with street lighting, curbing and guttering — the speed limit is 60 kmh. Outside built-up areas, as on country roads and highways, the general speed limit is 100kmh or 110kmh. Speeds of more or less than these limits may apply and the motorist is told by frequent restriction signs showing the highest speed applicable in that zone.

UNDER THE AFFLUENCE OF INKAHOL...

Eradication of drink-driving and related deaths is a national obsession. The State and Territory Governments seem to be competing with each other for the toughest approach to the problem of policing drink-driving. Random **breath testing** is the main road safety weapon. Only Scandinavia and Northern Ireland have more fanatical crusades to stamp out drink-driving offences. Critics of the policy say the almost puritanical campaign to stop people mixing drinking with driving is a political ploy. They say it is cheaper for the State Governments to run emotive publicity campaigns and provide more 'booze buses' (breath-testing units) than it is for them to build wider, safer roads and maintain them.

On the other hand, supporters point to facts and figures indicating that, since random breath-testing was pioneered by the State of Victoria in 1976 and then in other parts of the country, road deaths have fallen markedly. And it seems Australia's generally hard-drinking population is willing to live with even tougher drink-driving laws in the coming years.

In 1986, Victoria was considering a law whereby police may enter the homes of drivers suspected of being over the limit, at 0.05 per cent of alcohol per 100ml of blood (0.08 in some other states) — without a warrant — and demand they come with them for a blood-alcohol test. Victoria has also drafted a law extending a zero-alcohol limit on people in their first probationary year as licensed drivers, to their second year. There has been talk of making it illegal for 'professional' motorists like taxi drivers, truck drivers and delivery drivers to show *any* trace of alcohol in their blood when on the job.

INSURANCE AND REGISTRATION

The States are responsible for the building and upkeep of their urban and outback roads and car registration fees paid by owners form part of this budget. 'Rego' (registration fee) is payable according to the type of vehicle and the expected wear and tear it will inflict on a State's or Territory's roads over the year. Details of licence laws and registration for vehicles brought into the country are provided later in this Chapter. Remember: foreign insurance policies are generally *not* applicable in Australia. It is illegal to drive a vehicle, caravan or trailer on any public road unless at least Third Party (Bodily Injury) Insurance is in force to cover that vehicle, caravan or trailer effective in the State or Territory where it is to be driven.

Third Party Insurance

Third party insurance is compulsory throughout Australia. This is built into registration fees for automobiles and motorbikes paid to the States. Insurance for vehicles generally is not compulsory. It is calculated by private or government insurers on a zonal basis, depending on the region where the individual or business using the vehicle is based. Naturally, that risk is greater and premiums higher in city or urban areas where traffic is most heavy and accidents or thefts more likely to occur. For a private car, insurance and registration costs close to $A500 a year. People temporarily importing vehicles into the country are advised to extend their insurance for full cover in Australia.

Temporary visitors

In most States and Territories temporary residents and visitors are exempt from paying vehicle registration fees as long as the registration of that vehicle remains valid (unexpired) in the country of origin. As soon as possible after the vehicle has arrived in an Australian State or Territory it must be inspected by the nearest registration authority to make sure it is roadworthy. The documents required will include

- a *Carnet de Passage* or other evidence that security has been lodged with Customs authorities in Australia (see Chapter 15) **Taking It All With You** on customs and excise for immigrants.
- evidence that Third Party Insurance covers it in Australia
- a current registration certificate in the home country
- a valid driving licence for the would-be driver from his/her country of origin

MOTORING ORGANISATIONS, PETROL AND ROAD SERVICES

Most Australians belong to private motoring organisations. Some 60 to 75 per cent of car owners — twice the rate in Europe — find it pays to join the motoring organisation in their state or territory. The efficiency of the breakdown and rescue services provided by these associations is among the best in the world. Mechanics are at the scene within an hour of a member's telephone call to their base in some 80 per cent of cases. Fees are low in comparison to motoring organisations in other countries due to the high penetration of the market. Tourism literature, including free hotel guides and maps, as well as access to the motoring organisation's mechanic to check a used car the member is proposing to buy, are other attractions of becoming a member.

Petrol
Petrol prices vary by a few cents between the States, and in 1986-87 the average retail price for super fuel was less than 55 cents a litre. LPG and other grades of fuel are also available at Australia's service stations, and most provide spare parts and mechanical assistance. On day trips and driving holidays, the petrol stop can serve multiple purposes. But beware — the standard of comfort and service diminishes with the distance from civilisation. In the long hauls between towns, a hamlet often consists of a couple of petrol pumps, a garage where you pay for the petrol and (perhaps) a pub. The 'restaurant' and other facilities in Australia's isolated areas can be truly appalling, especially if the motorist is accustomed to the hi-tech finesse of American or European road rest centres.

BUY IT THERE OR BRING YOUR OWN?

If you're thinking about buying a car or other vehicle in Australia, new or second hand, the weakness in the 'Pacific Peso' against the currencies of Japan, the United States, West Germany, Italy and other major vehicle exporting nations means ever-steeper car prices in Australia. Tariffs and duties (to protect profits and jobs at local car manufacturing plants) were around 20 per cent in 1987 for models with wholesale prices above about $A20,000. So your car may well be worth taking with you to Australia, even after the high cost of transporting it there (as indicated in Chapter15 **Taking It All With You**). Otherwise you may be better off selling it before you leave; you could spend the money saved on vehicle shipment and customs on one bought in Australia when you arrive.

The market for prestige European cars in Australia is small but vigorous. European models dominate the expensive end of the market. Cars common on EEC roads like BMWs, Mercedes, Fiats, Renaults and Citroens turn heads in Australia because everyone knows they cost a small fortune. But servicing and spare parts can be tricky and expensive for such models, another factor to consider if you're trying to decide whether to take yours with you or buy one there.

Although just 12 per cent of all the new cars sold in Australia in 1986 were imports, the profits made on them are high enough to keep dealers smiling. Most imported models cost over $A100,000 new — double that for a Rolls Royce. In fact, during 1987 the Italian car maker Maserati decided there was space for the sleek Bi Turbo models Down Under and zoomed in alongside Porsche and Ferrari at the top end of the prestige car market. Overall, Mercedes-Benz is the most popular of the imported status cars, followed by BMW, Volvo, US-made Ford, Mazda and Jaguar.

If you are not satisfied with the Australian models, the Japanese or other imports from the Asian region represent top value for money. The companies which build or assemble vehicles at plants in Australia are Toyota, Mitsubishi, Nissan, General Motors Holden and Ford. The last two are long-established as the bigget-volume sellers on the new and used car market in Australia, providing easy access for repairs and parts at most car shops and garages. A locally assembled car in Australia will cost at least $A12,000 new (at 1987 prices).

Second hand cars

You can buy second hand vehicles privately. Australian newspapers have hefty sections advertising cars for sale from their owner-drivers, or from licensed dealers. Most big towns and cities have second hand car dealers concentrated in a particular area, while auction rooms also provide opportunities to pick up a fine vehicle minus a dealer's profit margin. If you're planning to buy a used car in Australia, it is wise to join the regional motoring organisation first so you can use one of its qualified mechanics to run an impartial check on a vehicle you might decide to purchase, in case it's not all it's hyped up to be.

Apart from obvious mechanical problems or other defects like rust, buying a stolen or debt-ridden car is a major trap. As a safeguard, all car dealers and auction rooms are obliged by law to provide title guarantees proving the vehicle is free of debt and not stolen. If you are buying privately through newspapers or personal contacts, legal points like these should be clarified first.

Car salespeople can be as slippery in Australia as elsewhere in the world, especially in highly competitive markets like Sydney's 'magic mile of motors' along the Parramatta Road. When closing a deal with a used car dealer, never put your signature to a purchase form until it is fully filled out and do not agree to a deal offering a free vehicle check. This 'free' check by the local automobile association will only be carried out *after* your signing of the purchase document; you could find yourself stuck with the vehicle irrespective of faults discovered. Even a purchase agreement subject to a satisfactory finding by the mechanical check should not be signed. Unless the terms of 'satisfactory' are well defined, you could find yourself in dispute with the dealer over the repair of any faults which do come to light.

Anyone foolish enough to pay a deposit and sign a purchase agreement before the mechanical testing is done, risks losing their money if they decide to scrap the deal. Some States stipulate a 'cooling off period' in the used car warranty, giving the buyer an option to return the vehicle within a certain period should it not be as represented by the dealer. Often used cars bought from dealers and costing more than a couple of thousand dollars will have some form of mechanical warranty as well.

THE LICENCE — FOREIGN AND AUSTRALIAN DRIVERS

Usually, a driver from abroad is allowed to drive on a current foreign or international licence for a 'period of grace' — after which he or she must take a local licence as a resident of a State or Territory. Most States and Territories license resident drivers yearly, and a licence fee is imposed each time as a revenue-raising tactic by governments. In some places the yearly fee can be paid in advance for a number of years, saving the annual hassle of renewing the permit. If you obtain a licence in one Australian State or Territory it is valid everywhere you drive inside the country. Similarly, if you are convicted of an offence, fined or otherwise penalised in one place, such convictions or unpaid fines also 'travel'. Sophisticated computer systems in most transport and police departments mean that the authorities will eventually catch up with you at the address on your licence.

It raises the hackles of many citizens that foreign diplomats and their dependants are immune from the obligation to pay the price of their traffic offences since as representatives of another government, they cannot be sued. People on diplomatic passports may be able to get away with non-payment of fines and minor offences, but there have been some ugly cases of driving incidents causing a political fracas between Australia and the country represented by the offending diplomat (or family member). There's continuing agitation for this aspect of diplomatic immunity to be tightened.

Though many States allow newcomers to get behind the wheel for a few months on the strength of a foreign licence, it is a good idea to take the initiative: study a summary of driving regulations from your local authority on arrival. Information may be obtained from the traffic authority in that State or Territory, its department of transport or motoring organisations.

12
Playing Down Under

NATURE — THE MIXED BLESSING

Fans of Australia agree you can't beat the local sun, sea, bush, snow and water sports for a good time. But whether you are at home or on a day out, sunburn, the flies, ants, mozzies (mosquitoes) and other biting insects make the outdoor life a mixed blessing. The aroma of coconut suntan oil and fumes of bug killer are as evocative of a dinky-di day as surf boards on the roof rack and a well-stocked eskie (box for keeping drinks cold) by the barbie.

Inland, as well as on the coast where most people live, Australia is remarkable for the proliferation of public barbeque places. It is hard to find a large or scenically located park without built-in facilities for cooking and picnics. Even roadside truckstops and rest areas usually have fireplaces to sizzle a steak or boil the 'billy'.

However, clearing your space of the previous occupants' litter can be a chore. Australians are not the tidiest people on earth, though in some places you can't see the kangaroos for the litter bins. On a sunny Sunday 'arvo' every family and their dog seems to be out and about. City beaches, or local dams, rivers and public swimming pools are often full of other people flocking to enjoy themselves. Those hoping to discover an isolated picnic setting with vacant facilities (tables, benches, fireplace, toilets and car parking) can be in trouble. But on weekdays parks, beaches and bushland in population centres are often quiet and empty.

Similarly, camping holidays in the national parks throughout the countryside and on the coast tend to be frenetic during weekends, school vacations or on public holidays — and peaceful the rest of the time. Australia's national parks usually have thoughtfully organised facilities for campers, while rangers from the local parks and wildlife service drop by to keep an eye on things. If you want to indulge a desire for splendid isolation and wander far enough afield in the off-season, it is possible to see no other human being for days — just possums, kangaroos, wallabies, lizards great and small as well as emus, kookaburras, magpies or shyer creatures like koalas and wombats.

BUGS AND BITES

Living Down Under also means putting up with bugs of the multi-legged variety. Unlike countries with cool climates, where only mice and rats survive indoors all year round, it is common for humans to share their homes with a multitude of bugs. Yet the presence of assorted species of flies, ants, spiders, moths and cockroaches inside a house doesn't necessarily mean its owners are slobs who leave a lot of exposed food around. Hot weather and bright lights are especially attractive to insect life — and the reason why wire mesh outside doors and windows is standard. To discourage insects and for general reasons of hygiene, it is particularly important in Australia to keep cupboards and surfaces scrupulously clean, and food in the refrigerator. Outdoors, this means taking insect repellent as part of your picnic, beach or gardening kit.

The reptile population

Apart from ubiquitous flying and biting insects, a few poisonous species of spiders and snakes may be found lurking in dark corners of a house, shed or garage as well as in gardens, urban parks and, naturally, in the bush.

Australia has a wide variety of lizards, many quite weird and even angry-looking but none are venomous; only the largest — the estuarine crocodiles of northern Australia — are dangerous. Since these 'crocs' bite you should not swim randomly in the creeks, rivers or waterholes of northern Queensland and the Northern Territory. The most dangerous of Australia's snakes are the brown snake, the tiger snake, the taipan and the death adder. Poisonous species of insect include the red back and trap-door spiders. However, these creatures are extremely shy and unlikely to be a hazard unless threatened. Fortunately, young children are taught at school about the venomous species in their environment. But newcomers of all ages should learn what these look like, from reference books at municipal libraries or in visits to zoos. If you are keen on bushwalking or have young children, in particular, it is important to know how to react in an encounter, and administer basic first aid.

Marine menaces

Sharks abound in coastal waters of Australia, though most popular coastal beaches have a surf watch to monitor their presence. Major beaches have shark netting to keep the monsters at bay. At patrolled beaches, when an unwelcome fin is spotted, shark alarms will alert people not to swim in the ocean. Similarly, beaches may be closed if the number of jelly fish is high. Walking along the shore, it is not uncommon to see bluebottles or other types of stinging jellies washed up — indicating what may be in store for a bather or paddler in an unguarded moment.

However, only a few of Australia's famous beaches can be regularly patrolled. As with land creatures, learn to recognise the types of sea life which are poisonous. Broadly, dangerous species to be found swimming beside you or underfoot in Australia's warm tropical oceans are the box jellyfish, the Portuguese Man'o'War and the stonefish of the Great Barrier Reef. Rock pools in eastern Australia are sometimes inhabited by the blue-ringed octopus. Venom from any of these may be fatal.

Fires

Inland Australia is notorious for grass and bushfires. It is imperative that people starting a fire in the bush do so only when and where signposts permit, while smokers should never throw smouldering matches or butts out of car windows into the scrub. Anyone who has seen the forests of charred tree stumps — not to mention the terror of actually being caught in a bush fire — knows the awesome consequences.

CITY LIFESTYLES — THE CONSUMER LANDSCAPE

More than 60 per cent of the population live, work and study in Australia's southern and coastal cities — from Brisbane south to Sydney, then Melbourne, and west to Adelaide and Perth. The spread of suburbs is daunting; Australia has some of the most sprawling urban centres in the world, with plenty of room for consumer facilities and individual housing beyond the compact high-rise of city centres. The suburbs are studded with backyard swimming pools, sports fields, modern shopping complexes, parks and children's playgrounds. Sydney and Melbourne, home for three to four million people each, cover about the same amount of ground as cities like Greater London or New York. From the air you can see wave after wave of detached bungalows, extending thousands of miles along the coast and inland, hemmed by mountain ranges.

FOOD

At a café in Florence, Italy, a blond Aussie breasted the bar. "A cup of cheeno, mate," he told the man behind the espresso machine. What the youth desired was a 'cappucinno', and though unable to pronounce it, he was sufficiently multicultured to know what he was talking about. Australians are accustomed to espresso machines, coffee grinders and continental experts at the controls. They enjoy access to the most cosmopolitan range of food and drink in the world.

This happy state of affairs was largely achieved in a decade or two. Many not-so-new Australians remember a time when it was difficult to buy anything but basic beans, peas, carrots and beef in Australia. But be prepared: in some places circumstances have not changed much. In the suburbs and country towns you can expect cafés offering 'Chinese and Australian' menus — meaning sweet'n'sour pork served with slimy potato chips. While excellent continental cake and coffee shops abound in big cities, the notorious 'Australian' cakeshops and milkbars are still in business, serving cups of cheeno made with Nescafé, dessicated lamingtons (sponge cake coated with chocolate and coconut) and similar horrors. Then there are the myths that in Australia everyone eats steaks for breakfast. Unless you work at an abattoir or on a cattle station and get plenty of cheap red meat, most people either can't afford it — or wouldn't want to swap their 'breakie' of muesli for a steak, anyway.

Though the Federal Government has effectively discouraged expense-account lunching and dining by removing tax concessions for business entertainment, eating out remains a national pastime. The restaurant industry flourishes on the basis of high disposable incomes, plenty of rural capacity to produce the necessary ingredients, and ethnic cooking styles imported by newcomers or by better-travelled restaurateurs.

Melbourne, Sydney and Adelaide have reputations for the best quality and highest number of restaurants per capita. Italian, Greek, French, Eastern European, Spanish, South American and Middle Eastern cuisines flourish. There seems to be a Chinese or other Asian restaurant in every main shopping centre. Sydney and Melbourne have impressive China Towns rivalling those of the larger American cities. Most Australians know and love the varieties of South-East Asian and other Oriental cuisines, due to prevailing high standards and low prices of such restaurants. Oriental food is to Australians what Indian is to the English, or Mexican to Californians.

Aussie cuisine

There is a reputedly 'Australian' cuisine — usually featuring wonderful local seafoods like crayfish, barramundi, John Dory and king prawns and exotic tropical fruits. The recipes and presentation are often a hybrid of French and South-East Asian styles. Less common are restaurants specialising in bush cooking, using ingredients considered great tucker by Aboriginals. Exotica like roast witchetty grubs served on a bed of alfalfa sprouts with peanut sauce, emu egg omlettes, and sweet pies made from little known native fruits like quandongs — are about as Australian as a broad-minded market can tolerate.

WINE AND BEER

More than a century ago fine wines started being produced in Australia. As long ago as the Vienna Exhibition of 1873 the 'Bruce Juice' up for tasting (actually Hermitage from Victoria) won first prize. When the European judges were told the wine was Australian, they thought again. Such wine could only be French, they insisted — and gave first prize to someone else.

Nowadays the quality of the Australian product is taken for granted. Much time and effort has been invested to make sure the world knows that Aussies are good for more than a beer and a barbie. At home, the market for wine is as big as for beer and far more prestigious. One West Australian millionaire even flew a full symphony orchestra from London to his vineyard south of Perth, for an open-air concert to help proclaim the establishment's achievements in winemaking.

Driving tours of winegrowing districts are ideal for getting to know Australia's regions and their wines. Its 'big three' wine labels, Penfolds, Lindermans and Orlando, have cellars and vineyards around the country. However, the best and most interesting wines are produced by family run boutique wineries. These are a pleasure to visit, and often have excellent restaurants as well.

The main grape-growing regions — the Barossa, Coonawarra and Clare Valley districts of South Australia, the Hunter Valley north-west of Sydney, the Rutherglenn area of Northern Victoria, and the Margaret River and Swan River Valley of South-Western Australia — produce wines that please even the most pernickety European palates. The best-known styles are Chardonnay, Semillon, Cabernet, Cabernet-Sauvignon and Shiraz. Australian fortified wines are highly regarded as well. Aussie wines are generally robust compared to the wines of Europe, so can be a shock to the system. In Australia, appreciation of their quality and range is so great that local labels predominate. Table wines in the Aussie-invented 'bladder' box are so popular that local 'grog shops' and 'bottle-Os' seem to be constructed of them. Unpretentious but quaffable plonk is certainly as good value for money as local table wines in France, Germany, Spain or Italy. However, boxed or bottled wine is not as cheap Down Under due to regular tax hikes on all kinds of alcoholic drinks mentioned earlier. But Australian champagne is an inexpensive treat compared to the price of the French original in Europe.

Beer

The Aussie wine boom notwithstanding, beer-drinking remains as popular as Paul Hogan. Like Hoges in one of his beer advertisements, beer lovers may well stand around in wine cellars complacent with a tinny while 'winos' spit their drinks out.

Of course beer drinkers are well-catered for in Australia, though it is often served so cold you can barely taste the stuff. Each State and even region produces beers boasting different qualities. Hot weather provides a perfect excuse to drink the stuff like water, often from iced glasses called schooners (pints) and middies (halves). The pubs make a feature of their beer gardens. Small inner-city establishments may call a plain concrete square the 'garden'; nonetheless drinkers and diners flock outdoors whenever possible, in the sun or under the stars.

Licensing laws

Licensing laws are less puritanical than in some Anglo societies, though not as liberal as in many parts of Europe. The cost of a liquor licence means that many Australian restaurants post a BYO (Bring Your Own) sign and charge a small amount for corkage (opening bottles and providing glasses). This is a great advantage, since restaurant wine menus can be pricey. Pubs and liquor retail hours have been liberalised in recent years, though varying from State to State. Beer, wine and spirits can be bought by people over the age of 18 from licensed shops, pubs or restaurants. Hotel (pub) trading is usually from 10am to 10pm Monday to Saturday and from noon to 8pm on Sundays.

THE ARTS AND ENTERTAINMENT

As in most affluent societies there is no shortage of opportunities for people to enjoy ballet, opera, music and any other entertainment they fancy. Australia's geographical isolation has sometimes been cited as a problem in popularising traditional artforms. It also has advantages — Australians have been forced to rely on local entertainers and so a vigorous cultural life with many talented artists has evolved.

Opera, ballet, modern dance, theatre, classical and pop music have strong followings and originality since Australians interested in the arts cannot always rely on regular injections of ideas and trends from overseas.

The arts, theatre and music are fostered by governments at Federal, State and local levels. Corporate sponsors also like to have their names associated with the arts and pour in millions of dollars to fund performances. Australians have money to spend on entertainment and theatre, music, art galleries and so forth vie with each other to attract an audience. Despite strictures imposed in favour of local talent by the entertainers' union, Actors' Equity, stars from other countries find it increasingly worthwhile to include Australia on their itinerary. Record shops and libraries in most cities and many towns are as well-stocked with music and video materials as any wealthy Western society. Facilities for performances have improved vastly in the past ten years, with major cities opening large entertainment complexes and concert centres.

Then there's the **Sydney Opera House**. Its acoustics and parking facilities may not be perfect, yet as a venue it is comparable to La Scala in Milan, the Carnegie Hall in New York or Covent Garden in London. The calibre of productions and standard of Australian opera, ballet and orchestras is often as good as anywhere else. Nevertheless, the wondrous harbour outlook as you sip champagne — or beer — at interval is as much part of the pleasure as what goes on inside its various halls.

Most State capitals are visited by big names from abroad, and many have their own theatre and opera companies, dance troupes, music academies, symphony orchestras and so on. Melbourne has the most vigorous theatre scene — conventional and fringe.

Pop culture

Popular music runs the gamut, from bush ballads to head-banging heavy metal. Bigger towns and cities have a wide range of venues or even entire neighbourhoods renowned for pubs, bars and restaurants featuring live rock, jazz, blues or folk music by local and international stars.

Australia's television culture is a bland mix of British and American. Hence, made-in-Australia soap operas proliferate at home and can be seen abroad along with Dallas and Coronation Street. Cinemas and radio stations follow the trend set by television, providing as much imported pap as allowed by the regulations on Australian content.

However, growing national pride and the celebration of 200 years of Western cultural evolution adds to pressure by artists, performers and others keen for Australia to assert cultural independence. Many artists — be they musicans, painters, writers, dancers, comedians or actors — rely on local colour, politics and folklore. Sharp and inventive, they have a definite Aussie accent.

Films

Australia has gained international acclaim for its films — to the point where, in some places the labelling of a film as 'Australian' means it must be good. Recently as many as 40 feature films have been produced a year in Australia — from deadly serious historical classics like *Picnic at Hanging Rock* to zany comedies like Paul Hogan in *Crocodile Dundee*, and of course the *Mad Max* series which started life distinctly Australian and wound up Americanised. To the credit of some States and the Canberra administration, film commissions have been maintained to channel available public and private monies into the industry.

MEDIA

The Australian Broadcasting Corporation (ABC) and a handful of privately-owned networks dominate the market for television entertainment. Hundreds of radio stations — ABC, community or university-based as well as commercial 'stations — put even the most remote places on the air. Television is the most popular source of quick news, advertising and entertainment for the masses. Apart from the crass soapies, game shows and comedies of British, American or local origin already mentioned, Australians can tune into ethnic radio and television shows.

Critics of the publicly-funded multicultural broadcasting policy say the main difference between ethnic programming and shows of English or American origin is that they must endure irritating subtitles as well. There was a flurry when the government threatened to merge the Special Broadcasting Service with ABC. Until 1986 the SBS had been in charge of ethnic broadcasting. While some lamented the loss of a separate ethnic broadcasting authority, the mouthpiece of Australia's large Italian community, newspaper *Il Globo*, declared: "Basta! Enough...The SBS has offended the Italian community with idiotic, dated and offensive contents of its programs...it repeated ad nauseam films of the lowest category about prostitutes, pimps, drug addicts, the alienated, Mafia criminals, terrorists, scandalmongers, emphasising corruption, obscenity and blasphemy...SBS was managed by Anglo-Saxons insensitive to community needs...Their idea of local coverage was contests of spaghetti eaters with their hands tied behind their backs..."In 1987 it was decided that SBS would remain a separate entity in public broadcasting.

So the ethnic broadcasting experiment in Australia continues. From the intending immigrant's point of view it is important as a measure of the influence of New Australians in the community. Australia is even selling its subtitled ethnic television programmes in other countries. Newspapers and magazines written in English and other community languages — as well as in 'Orstralian' — proliferate. While the quality press sticks to formal English usage and reprints many articles syndicated from top publications in Britain and the US, Aussie 'dialect' has infiltrated popular newspapers and magazines.

In attitude, if not always in language, the local media is proudly — sometimes aggressively — Ocker.

On the airwaves, no effort is made by many popular broadcast and public personalities to supress the Aussie nasal twang and the success of political as well as media personalities these days owes much to that bloke/sheila-in-the-street approach. The trend to an 'Australian' sound among radio and television presenters means people struggling with the English language or simply accustomed to hearing BBC tones may not understand much of what is said.

News

Nevertheless, Australia's news and current affairs media often provide excellent services. Compared to many countries, and considering the time difference (9 to 11 hours ahead of Western Europe) and geographic isolation, Australia is well-catered for in terms of internatonal news. Words and pictures reach local papers, radio and television screens practically as soon as they happen in countries of origin. Partly due to the immigrant background of many Australians, foreign news and analysis feature prominently in the serious newspapers.

At the last count, Sydney had six major daily newspapers, Melbourne and Brisbane three each, while most other cities and larger towns had at least two. In addition, the suburbs and shires usually have privately-owned local papers. There are two newspapers available nationally for news and advertising every day — *The Australian* and *The Australian Financial Review*. This is quite a feat since the national dailies must be transported from regional printworks by road, air or rail all over the vast continent to achieve national circulation.

As well as stridently local magazines like *The Australian Woman's Weekly*, *Woman's Day*, *Dolly*, *New Idea* and *Sheila*, together with a number of radio and television support magazines, there are Down Under editions of *Vogue*, *Cosmopolitan* and *Time* while the *Bulletin* includes *Newsweek*. Control of the commercial broadcast and print media is in comparatively few hands, despite pressure by governments and other groups keen to loosen the stranglehold of companies like Rupert Murdoch's News Ltd, which controls 60% of the Australian media, Kerry Packer, Robert Holmes à Court and the Fairfax organisation (John Fairfax & Sons) who run much of the remainder. Australia's media chiefs are often blatantly involved in politics and openly use their publications or programmes to influence events. Many Australians are well aware that those in control of the media often do not restrain themselves from using their news services to further their own interests. Yet media bias is a burning issue only among a minority of the population. The rest ignore it, or use 'media bias' as an excuse for their lazy Aussie apathy about 'important' issues, 'cos y'd be a mug to believe everything in the news, wouldn't ya?'

COMMUNICATIONS

Due to the country's size, scattered population and isolation from its main trading partners, as well as the high standard of living, Australians have lavished much money and energy on acquiring the best technology to keep in touch with each other and everyone else. Its telephone system is run by the Federal Government-backed **Telecom** organisation; computerisation of communications is at a high level in comparison to most other countries. The launching of the AUSSAT satellite in the mid-1980s began a new era in national and international communications Down Under. Via AUSSAT, remote areas are able to receive broadcasts as well as making possible new services in areas like entertainment, education, aviation and defence. Information about foreign news, investment and commodities markets are available in an instant through international agencies and data banks.

The Telecom corporation is responsible for installing and leasing circuits for a wide range of purposes. International telephone and telex links are made via the **Overseas Telecommunication Commission** (OTC) using under-sea cables and satellites. Other OTC services include Overseasfax, a facsimile transmission service available to some 50 countries; MIDAS, an international packet-switching service giving its users access to world-wide databases and computer resources; MINERVA, an international electronic mail service; INTERPLEX, which provides customers with their own international private line exchange; and ITCNET, a private networking system giving subscribers exclusive use of part of an international telephone exchange for voice/data transmissions.

Both AAP-Reuter and AP-Dow Jones offer services for businesspeople to keep up with international trade, share, commodity and money markets through computer terminals on a 24-hour basis.

Telephones

Though Telecom instals direct dialling services (STD) for calls within Australia, its subscribers must make special arrangements for the international service (ISD), so operator-connected calls overseas remain the norm for most households and many businesses.

Many Australians are shocked when they make telephone calls in foreign countries and discover they must pay for both the duration and timing of local telephone calls. In Australia local telephone charges are the same, no matter how long the call takes or the time of day or night when it is made, though STD and ISD calls have fixed time/duration charges.

Mail

Australia Post is a public company which has sole responsibility for distributing and delivering all standard national and international mail.

However, some of its minor divisions, like parcel delivery and courier services, have been sold to private contractors in recent years who run express mail services. Meanwhile, Australia Post provides its 'priority paid' facility for next-day mail deliveries inside and outside Australia (applying to addresses in Britain, the US and a number of other countries with frequent flights from Australia).

SPORT AND HEALTH

"If you exercised and dieted and lived like me for *one month*, you'd be really fit..."

"Look mate, if you worked and drank and ate like me for *one day*, you'd be dead — so who's fit?"

With this dialogue an Australian magazine sums up a national schism in matters of health and exercise in a cartoon. Sure, many Aussies are obsessed with obtaining the sun-bronzed Bondi lifesaver image. They revel in a range of physical activities. On the other hand, anyone who goes to Bondi Beach must be prepared for the paucity of hunky lifesavers and bikini beauties. Like suburban folk in most countries, Australians tend to unsightly flab — not rippling muscles — beneath the national suntan.

A soft lifestyle means at least as many Australians exercise no more than their arm muscles (lifting glass to mouth, pulling poker machine handles, changing television channels) in their leisure hours. Heart disease is the nation's major cause of death, linked to over-rich diet, smoking and lack of exercise. They are naturally seduced by sunshine — equating a leathery tan with good health. The incidence of skin cancer among Australians is high.

Walking is the number one regular physical activity. According to a survey published in 1986, 46 per cent walk for fitness. Swimming, aerobics, running and cycling follow walking in popularity. Football and soccer, golf and tennis, netball and basketball are the other most popular physical activities among Australians, in order of preference.

Though even the most indolent Aussies agree sport is a generally healthy activity, they are most passionate about it as spectators. Sporting heroes and heroines are Australia's royalty, consuming an inordinate amount of space in the news. When Alan Bond's yachties wrested the America's Cup from the New Yorkers in 1983 a kind of hysterical joy gripped the country. People took the Perth team's triumph as their personal victory. Enthusiasm for the return bout off the waters of Perth in 1986-87 had as much to do with sport and patriotism as with grasping commercial opportunities through tourism and the mood was grim when they lost.

Footy

Cricket is the main summer sport, but many versions of 'footy' dominate the airwaves and news stands in winter. The most popular football games in Queensland and New South Wales are rugby league and rugby union. Though most team sports have a time and place in Australia, due to immigrants of so many backgrounds, the Australians have evolved their own brand of football — known as Aussie Rules.

Aussie Rules is most popular in Victoria, South Australia, Western Australia and Tasmania. It emerged in the mid -19th century and has evolved since the days of Irish immigrants to the Victorian goldfields, who based their game on Gaelic football and hurley. Its admirers say the players are wonderfully fit and macho, but detractors claim that this type of football is one of the most uncouth ever played — one step up from mud-wrestling. There are 18 men to a side, and the aim is to put the ball between four posts. Nobody gets sent off and the injured are left where they fall. Punching, kicking, or hitting the ball with any part of the body is allowed. The only no-no is tackling below the knee or above the shoulder. Victorious hulks hugging each other in the mud, blood spattered losers being dragged from the field by their mates — these are common sights in news reports of a day's big footy game.

SPORT AND GAMBLING

Sporting events can be relied upon to stir fierce emotions. Aussies are keen to put their money where their hearts lie — and lay their bets as gestures of loyalty, sporting spirit, or simply for the thrill. Armchair athletes abound. A flutter on the races is part of the Great Australian Way. The Melbourne Cup every November brings the country to a halt for a few minutes while the big horse race is run. For days in advance and afterwards the media stokes the public's fascination, detailing the international horsey people who'll be at Flemington Racecourse on the big day, which horses are running, an annual parade of flamboyant hats and high (as well as low) fashion among the socialites in attendance, the champagne parties before, during and after the horses have their five minutes in the spotlight. And there's hardly a club, office, or school where 'sweeps' on the current crop of top 'nags' running at Flemington have not been organised.

Australia is also unique for more offbeat sporting-cum-betting opportunities: cane toad races in northern Queensland, dwarf-throwing contests in certain regions, and send-ups of posh 'Pommy' socio-sporting occasions, like the annual Henley-on-Todd regatta at Alice Springs. This particular 'boat race' is a farcical version of the Henley-on-Thames affair in England, starring the top Oxbridge university rowing teams. In Pommyland's original version, champagne and real water flows. However, the Todd River is a very dry place in Central Australia where the favourite thirst quencher is, of course, beer. The locals of 'the Alice' lay bets, drink heavily and watch hordes of hairy legs (shorts are *de rigeur* in the desert heat) bearing 'boats' along the Todd course. The similarly facetious Beer Can Regatta at Darwin features vessels made of emptied, flattened tinnies, though the things are actually floated on water in this Ocker send-up of prestigious sailing events in Mother England and elsewhere.

13
Australian
Health and Welfare

AUSTRALIA — STATE OF WELFARE

In comparision to many Western countries, social security provisions are generous for low income earners, people who lose their jobs, single parents, widows, the aged, the retired, and anyone — poor or rich — needing urgent medical attention. Unlike many places, Australia offers long-term unemployment benefits to eligible people (citizens and, in some cases, permanent residents deemed to be genuinely unable to get work). On the medical side, 'free' (taxpayer-financed) care can be upgraded or replaced by a range of private funds and insurance facilities, if a person is prepared to buy into a scheme. The same applies to people wanting to arrange private superannuation packages for when they retire, which they may receive in addition to government pension payments.

Australia's public health and welfare system is paid for by Federal and State Governments, financed in turn by taxpayers. Some services are available to all people in Australia, irrespective of whether they be citizens, permanent/temporary residents or tourists. For instance, all migrants have a right to use the Australian public hospital and medical system, **Medicare**, and an obligation to pay the tax surcharge (levy) which helps the Federal Government finance the facilities. Almost anyone else with permission to stay in Australia longer than six months — even tourists from certain countries — may use Medicare too, and without having to pay the tax levy.

WHO CANNOT RECEIVE AUSTRALIAN WELFARE BENEFITS

However, as mentioned in the Chapter on entering Australia, some newcomers may not be able to take advantage of public health and welfare benefits. Permanent residence is often granted to people in the 'family reunion/migration' category who have a 'sponsor'. That sponsor may have agreed, in effect, to support a relative in Australia by signing an Assurance of Support. In the case of migrants who are the parents of such a sponsor and older than 55, for men, and 50, for women, that Assurance to the immigration authorities means the son or daughter is responsible. If the sponsored parent claims any such benefits the sponsor must repay the Federal, State, local government or non-government charity which provided them.

In addition, members of foreign diplomatic missions and their families are exempt from the public health care system; they must make their own arrangements for necessary treatment. Visitors and temporary residents from a country without a reciprocal pension agreement with Australia cannot claim welfare benefits and pensions, though they may qualify for emergency benefits or assistance.

RECIPROCAL SOCIAL SECURITY ARRANGEMENTS

Australia has agreed with Britain and New Zealand, to guarantee welfare benefits, pensions and health care to each other's citizens on a reciprocal basis. In 1987, Australia was negotiating arrangements with Austria and West Germany, while an agreement with Italy was completed in principle, but awaiting approval by respective parliaments before it could come into force.

Reciprocal agreements may take years to finalise. Australia faces particular complexities forging its agreements with other countries, due to the unique grounds it uses to decide whether people have welfare entitlements. In Australia, eligibility for pensions and benefits depends on residence and personal wealth (assets and income tests apply in most cases). By contrast, many European countries, for example, have national insurance systems which people pay into during their years in the workforce — and so earn entitlement to claim social security payments.

You would be wise to ask about your entitlements *before* you go to Australia from the social security authorities in your country of citizenship. Similarly, you should find out whether you must continue paying national insurance or equivalent contributions to your country of origin, if you are unlikely to qualify for pensions in Australia (see details later in this chapter, on pension entitlements).

If you are a British citizen, for example, the reciprocal agreement covers basic health and welfare in Australia even during a stay of six months or less. If, like Britain, your country has a reciprocal agreement with Australia and you are staying there long-term or are otherwise assessed as a 'permanent resident' for welfare purposes, most pensions and benefits may be claimed by you. In Britain's case, the reciprocal agreement means that, if paid a pension by your own country while in Australia — for example, an age pension — it will be 'topped up' by the Australian authorities if it is *less* than the current rate of an equivalent pension in Australia. But when an Assurance of Support has been signed by a sponsoring employer or relative, you may be effectively disqualified from being paid pensions and benefits in Australia, even if your country has a reciprocal agreement with Australia.

If your country has *not* completed such an agreement on social security payments, there are certain **emergency benefits** available to you in Australia if you are in great financial hardship. Otherwise, you can expect to depend on your pension entitlements from your country of origin if you have no other form of income during your time in Australia. However, if you have permission to stay in Australia more than six months — whatever your nationality — you are entitled to use the Medicare health care system. Some countries, like Britain, have arrangements for short-term visitors and tourists to use the 'free' public medical and hospital system in Australia.

International standards

Generally, Australia tries to apply certain standards to its arrangements with other countries on reciprocal social security agreements. Australia aims to ensure that pensions and benefits are payable and transferable under reciprocal agreements between Australia and other countries, and allows people to receive pensions from the different countries they have lived and worked in during their lifetimes. As an immigrant or temporary resident of Australia, you may benefit from this type of reciprocal agreement on welfare benefit if:

- you returned to your country of origin before becoming qualified to claim an age pension in Australia
- you have not lived and worked long enough in some other country to qualify for that country's pension
- you have lost your pension rights from your country of origin because you have ceased to be a citizen, are no longer resident there or because of currency restrictions

THE AUSTRALIA CARD

Although it had not come into force at the time of writing, the Australia Card system could be in operation by 1988 to ensure that Australians receive their due in terms of welfare and health services, as well as for checking in taxation and various financial transactions.

MEDICARE

Medicare is the name of Australia's current public hospital and medical insurance system and, until the Australia Card legislation is passed, it is necessary to register at a Medicare office in Australia to be eligible for benefits.

In Australia, policy on public health care hasn't evolved smoothly: it has been chopped and changed by successive governments. Federal administrations of conservative leanings (Liberal-National Country Party) have been — and would in future be — committed to a user-pays policy, with private health insurance being the only option for most people not in 'needy' circumstances. Until the early 1970s, this was the policy. Private funds flourished while the government looked after the bottom end of the market. The arrival of the reforming Labor Government of Prime Minister Gough Whitlam introduced a publicly-funded system known as **Medibank**. Its philosophy was that every Australian should have equal access to health care.

Medibank and Medicare

Medibank proved incredibly expensive and inefficient from the administrative viewpoint, though with the return to more conservative rule under Liberal Prime Minister Malcolm Fraser in 1975, the public was assured that Medibank would remain intact. For all its inefficiency, the concept of 'free' public health care (in fact paid for by a tax levy) appeared popular. But Medibank was gradually dismantled and the private health funds seemed to be back in business, catering to the needs of most people unwilling to take a risk on their health and the costs of falling ill, while the Government took care of low income earners.

With the return of a Labor Government in 1983, Medicare was introduced. Broadly, the principle of Medibank remained but the administrative details were changed to make it more economical. Taxpayers are obliged to contribute a proportion of their earnings (unless in low-income categories) as a levy to pay for Medicare services. By 1987, the Medicare levy was 1.25 per cent. If desired, private health insurance can be bought as well and the system leaves some scope for private funds to cover 'gaps' in medical and hospital extras. As well as public (government) hospitals and doctors who work primarily within Medicare, the services of Australia's many private hospitals and medical specialists are available to paying patients. If you have a chronic illness, and prefer to be treated or operated on by the doctor of your choice, private health insurance is advisable.

The **Health Insurance Commission** runs Medicare, and through its offices a card is issued to registered temporary and permanent residents.

You may also be eligible to use Medicare if you are a tourist with citizenship of a country that has a reciprocal agreement with Australia covering health care, on production of your passport. Britain has such an agreement. It is *not* necessary to enrol at a Medicare office as soon as you arrive in Australia. After you visit a doctor or a pharmacy for the first time and want to claim back any money you have paid for consultation, medicines or other eligible treatments, you can register with Medicare in order to receive your refund. Whether you wait before seeing a doctor or not, to register for Medicare you must fill in an application form, obtainable at a Medicare regional office or at post offices throughout Australia.

Medicare provides:

- accommodation in public hospitals and treatment by doctors appointed by the hospital at no charge to both in-patients and out-patients
- refunds of at least 85 per cent of the scheduled (government-approved) fee for each medical service provided by private doctors (at home or at a surgery). The 15 per cent paid by the patient is called the 'gap' and is refundable via private health insurance, if such insurance has been arranged. If the doctor charges more than the scheduled fee, the patient cannot claim a Medicare refund for that part of the cost. Some doctors do not charge the patient a fee, but bill the Government direct (bulk-billing)
- in the case of high-cost treatments such as operations, Medicare will pay all but a nominal part of the bill ('gap')
- where the 'gap' amounts to more than a certain amount ($A150 at time of writing) within any one financial year (July of one year to June of the following year) Medicare will refund 100 per cent of the scheduled fee for the remainder of the year
- the refund of 85 per cent of scheduled fee includes eye tests by optometrists
- cut-price pharmaceuticals, costing the individual no more than $A10 per prescription on the first 25 items a year, after which no charge is made.

The scheduled fees referred to in explaining Medicare services are set by an independent tribunal, which usually approves an increase once a year to absorb the impact of inflation on the doctors expenses in running their practices and related costs. At each visit to the doctor, the Medicare card (or Australia Card, if and when it is issued) should be produced for identification and administrative purposes. *Note:* None of the Medicare fees apply for treatment at a hospital, and bills are charged directly to the government.

Medicare does NOT provide:

- doctors' charges when higher than the scheduled fee or the remaining 15 per cent 'gap', if the doctor does not bulk bill the Government
- accommodation and treatment as a private patient (with the doctor of your choice, ex-Medicare) even if at a public hospital
- accommodation and treatment at a private hospital
- treatments by physiotherapists, chiropractors, and other non-medical practitioners
- ambulances
- dentists, though some oral surgery *is* refundable under Medicare
- medical repatriation
- funeral costs

Private health insurance

In order to compete with Medicare, private health funds offer a range of insurance packages to cover all of the above services, tailored to different pockets. Bear in mind that private health care and 'non-essential' operations, or hospital stays as a private patient, are expensive in Australia. Dental charges can be alarming, when you consider the likely needs of a young family or people facing extensive treatment.

Generally, the health funds provide packages at basic, intermediate and high levels of cover, calculated for members at single or family rates, payable at a fund office on a weekly basis or deductible from your salary by arrangement with a bank or employer. As a guide, figures published by the *Melbourne Age* newspaper in 1986 showed that a family of four living on a single income of average male earnings paid $A11.40 a week for basic insurance from a private fund, $A13.89 for intermediate cover and $A17.51 for-top level insurance. Services at basic, intermediate and top-level are described below.

At basic level, private health funds in Australia supplement Medicare with the choice of own doctor (private) at a public hospital. Intermediate insurance deals tend to offer refunds of a greater percentage of private hospital costs while top private insurance offers a large enough refund on private hospital rates to allow a patient to have an individual room. These packages also include dentistry and other exclusions from Medicare mentioned above.

MEDICARE OVERSEAS

As well as reciprocal health insurance arrangements with other countries, Medicare provides basic insurance for Australian residents when abroad. For people outside Australia no more than two years, refunds of medical expenses incurred overseas can be claimed even while the claimant is out of Australia, although hospital charges are not included. So it remains a good idea to take travel insurance when you travel out of Australia. Check with Medicare before you depart. Claims from Medicare can be made via Australian consular offices which supply the necessary forms. If you leave Australia for more than two years, you may not be eligible to claim refunds on medical treatment and should check with a Medicare office before leaving the country.

FAMILY ALLOWANCES

These allowances are paid once a month by cheque to all parents (or couples) and guardians looking after a child. There is no income or asset testing; the amount paid depends on how many children are in the family under the age of 16. After children turn 16, the allowances is paid only for those who are full-time students and *not* earning more than a set amount from a part-time job. Family allowances are also claimable for children aged 18 to 24 if the parent or guardian is eligible for:

- additional payment for a student under another government pension, benefit or allowance
- family income supplement, or has an income below the minimum limits set for the supplement
- payment for a student from an orphan's pension, handicapped child's allowance, Aboriginal secondary grants scheme, isolated children's scheme (if income tested) or any of the Commonwealth schemes named by the Department of Social Security.

At the time of writing, the rates for family allowances were about $A23 a month for one child, $A56 a month for two children, $A95 a month for three children and $A134 a month for four children. As well, there are special payments in addition to the regular family allowances in the case of multiple births. These are payable until the children are six years old, providing three or more survive; at $A150 a month (at time of writing) for triplets; at $A200 a month (at time of writing) for quads or higher multiples. No special payments are made for twins.

14
Australian Education

Australians are all required to go to school from the time they are six until they finish junior high school at about the age of 15. However, the pressures of a specialised technological society — not to mention unemployment and uncertainty about the consequences of a too-hasty exit from school — mean that Australians commonly continue formal education well into young adulthood. Yet they are not as keen on gaining education and job skills as other Western countries: according to a survey quoted in the *Economist* in 1987, Australia was bottom of the OECD league table (except for Spain, New Zealand and Portugal) in vocational training and apprenticeships.

Nevertheless, Australia still manages to make big news with its breakthroughs in everything from test tube babies to the Sarich orbital engine (a low-fuel car invented by a Yugoslav immigrant). Though comprising only 0.03 per cent of the world's population, the Aussies write 2 per cent of the world's scientific papers, win 1.3 per cent of Nobel prizes and make 0.7 per cent of the world's patent applications. (The *Economist*, March 1987).

This Chapter is a guide for parents of young families and people intending to educate their children in Australia, or people of *any* age planning to continue their own education when they go to live in Australia.

SCHOOLDAYS — WOT'S IN AN OLD SCHOOL TIE ANYWAY?

About 75 per cent of school-age children attend 'free' (tax-paid) government institutions. The rest are sent to preparatory, primary and secondary schools run by religious, sectarian or non-denominational private organisations. Confusingly for people from other English-speaking backgrounds, the term **public school** in Australia means a government school (open to the general public). Non-government schools are usually known as **private** schools.

Private schools

But there is rarely any snobbery about which school a person attended and little or no kudos attached to private education. In some places, education at a particularly well-funded, high-standard government school is preferred to most exclusive private colleges. Dropping the name of an expensive private school rarely means much to anybody, beyond the rarified atmosphere of the most snooty establishment drawing rooms. Around the 'barbie', you are more likely to make a social splash with an account of the footy club you played for in your youth, than by dropping the name of the institution where you spent your formative years. The inclusion of certain private schools on your curriculum vitae may help to gain employment — but usually due to a fine academic reputation, rather than any attraction to 'old school tie' values. Compare this to Britain where 'Old Harrovian', 'Rodean Hockey Captain' or 'Westminster Old Boy' are bandied about in conversation and gossip columns to define otherwise undistinguished individuals.

One reason for the lack of snobbishness about education in Australia is that children do not always come away from private schools with better accents, a 'born to rule' ambition or anything else to set them above their mates. When the public school down the road seems to offer a similar product, Shirlene's ballet lessons or fixing Craig's buck teeth at the orthodontist may be sounder investments than spending thousands of dollars on private education.

Private boarding schools

Another explanation for this egalitarian approach to education is that, among the upwardly-mobile classes, to have attended a boarding school is the exception, not the rule. The predominance of private *day* schools over *boarding* schools means that relationships forged at school are perhaps less intense. Private day education does not provide the club aura of boarding school, where members eat, sleep and play together as well as attending classes. Opportunities for group discipline are also reduced by the day school environment. As at government institutions, teachers often have trouble enforcing the rules about students' uniforms (boaters, ties, gloves, even kilts are part of private school rig) and orderly conduct. A private (day) school in Australia is merely a workplace, not a club — or prison — for an élite.

Pupils at boarding schools are usually there because they are from outback areas, or their parents work overseas. Such students may even have the sympathy of their peers, since they cannot escape the watchful eyes of teachers by returning home each day.

However, it is in the range of subjects and extra-curricular activities that Australia's 2,500-odd private day and boarding schools shine. The teacher/pupil ratio may also be better. Some private schools, especially those run by Catholic orders or the local diocese, are highly dependent on grants from the Government, have few special facilities but are relatively cheap to attend. However, most private schools *are* expensive; they commonly charge $A1500 a year or more at high school level (double that for boarding schools). Books, uniforms, excursions, and equipment are extra. In order to attract bright pupils to enhance their academic reputations, many private schools offer part or full scholarships.

Your choice

A decision on public versus private education may depend on the special facilities you want for your child, like religious instruction or — as in the case of some ethnic community schools — non-English languages. There are schools run by the gamut of religious and ethnic groups: Anglican, Baptist, Christian Scientist, Greek Orthodox, Jewish, Muslim, Hare Krishna. There are also 'alternative' schools which offer free development for pupils, rather than structured classes, uniforms and conventional discipline.

As in government schools, the trend at private schools is away from single-sex education.

HOURS, COURSES AND WHO PAYS FOR WHAT

The school day, whether at a public (government) or private establishment, is on a par with standard working hours in Australia, though slightly shorter. There is no long 'siesta' as in some countries, nor are classes commonly stopped after lunch — they start at about 9 am and continue with a break for lunch and 'recesses' mid-morning and mid-afternoon, until around 4 pm. The school year starts in February; it has three or four terms depending on the State or Territory in charge, and ends in December for Christmas holidays, lasting about two months. There are also holidays of a week or more between terms. Public holidays and long weekends punctuate schooldays as well.

Schoolchildren are expected to do homework and may volunteer or be obliged to attend extra recreational or academic activities outside the 9 to 4, Monday to Friday timetable. Outdoor and water sports, in particular, are important additions to scheduled activities in a land where the climate is so conducive to all the physical pursuits under the sun.

Languages, computer studies, home sciences, arts and crafts are a feature of an Australian government school education. Learning methods rely on discussion and research rather than repetition, parrot-fashion. Within a subject syllabus, teachers at government and most private schools enjoy some freedom from rigid examination requirements (see later in this Chapter) to tailor lessons to the interest and level of their pupils.

Fees

Private schools charge fees of $A1,000 to $A1,500 a term—a lower figure for primary pupils—and rising as the pupil progresses through high school to **matriculation** (the necessary entry qualification for Australian universities and colleges of advanced education discussed later in this Chapter). Fees at private schools are usually payable per term. As mentioned above, many private schools offer scholarships to pupils assessed by examinations or otherwise to be academically or otherwise gifted, and so likely to add to the reputation of that establishment.

Government schools charge no tuition fees. However, they are not free of charge to parents. Books, uniforms (less comprehensive than for private schools), excursions, calculators, school bags, donations to school fêtes and charities, transport to and from school, computer studies fees, art and craft equipment and other 'incidentals' considered standard must be paid for. A recent survey of 2,000 government schools in New South Wales showed that parents paid an average of $A265 per child in years 1 and 2 for such incidentals — *not* including uniforms. The same survey, by the Federation of Parents' and Citizens' Organisations, estimated the cost of sending a child to primary schools was about $A180 a year, and secondary schooling at $A390 a year.

The sign of a good government school is an effective **Parents' and Citizens' Association (PCA)**. Each public school has such a body, to give parents a say in the running and upgrading of the establishment. They may run 'tuck-shops' where children are sold lunches and snacks, organise fêtes, fairs and other fund-raising events to buy the equipment that the State Department of Education cannot finance.

Pupils of government schools throughout Australia are encouraged to wear winter and summer uniforms. Secondhand items may be supplied through the PCA to families unable to pay shop prices for new uniforms.

Teachers are trained and hired by the Government. Their pay rates are generally on a par with the national average but are often the envy of their friends since they have shorter hours and longer holidays. School facilities are maintained and expanded by the State or Territory Government, with some contribution from the Federal Department of Education.

Exercise books and writing equipment are supposed to be supplied by parents. Some States provide textbooks free to primary school students and, at higher levels, most State and Territory Governments subsidise the cost of textbooks. Subsidies for books are paid directly to parents or to the school where a pupil in enrolled. The parents of pupils in the final two years of secondary school (prior to matriculation to university or higher education) may apply for **means-tested grants** administered by the Federal Government. There are a number of other allowances for children from low income families. Special payments may be made to children who must live away from home to attend school or study at home by correspondence because they are disadvantaged by geographic isolation, physical or intellectual disabilities. Government financial aid and subsidies for textbooks and equipment are increased now and then, to maintain their value in the face of rising living costs.

PRE-SCHOOL AND CHILD CARE

Local, State and Federal Governments have comprehensive child care programmes; the demands on the time of parents, single or otherwise, as in any Western society are great. In Australia, 30 per cent of mothers with children up to age 4 are in paid jobs. Access to a day nursery or kindergarten is an important social and political issue in Australia, and in crowded suburbs, despite the existence of government pre-schools finding a day care centre with room for your toddler can be tough. Fees are charged even by the government establishments though low income families may be exempt. Otherwise, it costs at least $A12 a week to send a child to a public day care centre. The greater the parent's income, the more he or she may be asked to pay for the child.

However, government pre-schools are usually free, though parents may be asked to pay a levy voluntarily. They take children aged between 3 and 6, are often attached to primary schools and are open during school terms. Morning or afternoon sessions are available. Pre-schools, also known as 'kindergarten' in the year before the child starts primary school, are intended to provide a basis for reading and numeracy skills, as well as physical, social and emotional preparation for the child's next 12 years or so in school.

PRIMARY SCHOOL

In New South Wales, Victoria, Tasmania and the Australian Capital Territory, primary school years begin at Year 1 and end at Year 6. In South Australia and the Northern Territory there is an extra year in pre-school, while Queensland and Western Australian pupils have an additional year in primary school before they qualify for high school. It is not compulsory to send a child to primary school until he/she is 6, though often children start attending at the age of 5. Most States enrol new pupils in February, the start of the school year, though the Northern Territory and South Australia offer continuous enrolments.

Government schools account for 80 per cent of primary age pupils in Australia. Classes average about 30 pupils and boys and girls are expected to attend lessons together. Generally, one teacher will be in charge of a class for the year, though a special teacher may take lessons in sports or craftwork, for example.

The class teacher guides pupils through a wide range of subjects, including language, arts, mathematics, elementary science, music, health and physical education. Religious education is optional at most State schools. Continuous assessments and reports to parents of each child's intellectual and social progress take the onus off the end of year examination to show how the individual is faring.

Sex education is widely taught, except in Queensland. Parents' permission may be sought for the teaching of this subject and others, like religion, or those which involve extra cost, like some sports and day trips.

Swimming lessons are a feature of suburban life for children. Basic swimming and, later, more advanced life-saving skills or water sports are taught from primary school during supervised sessions at public swimming pools. Wealthier private schools and even some government schools have their own swimming pools.

If pupils' families move from one district to another, they are expected to change to a school nearer their new home.

SECONDARY SCHOOLS

At the age of 12 or 13, children are transferred to a local government **high school** (or Secondary School, as it is also known). This is the stage when many parents decide the time is right for a transfer to a private school, if facilities there are considered superior. The four to six years of secondary school are crucial for building on skills and knowledge acquired in primary school, so the individual can choose and gain entry to further education and make his/her own way in society.

In New South Wales, Victoria, Tasmania and the Australian Capital Territory, secondary education lasts from Year 7 to Year 12. In other States, the starting point is known as Year 8 and ends at Year 12. However, in private schools the terminology may be different. At high school level many private schools refer to class 'years' as 'forms'. For example first form is equivalent to Year 7/8 (age 12 or 13) while the final year students before matriculation are usually 'sixth formers'.

Pupils entering government high schools are not subject to **streaming** in academic or technically oriented institutions, as in some countries. However, Victoria does provide a choice between university-oriented schools and **technical high schools**, slanted towards preparing pupils for careers in skilled trades or sub-professional courses by placing greater emphasis on practical and craft subjects.

On the whole, secondary schools cater for a diversity of personal and employment aspirations though some States have certain high schools specialising in agricultural or commercial subjects which may not be available at government or even private schools.

EXAMINATIONS AND ASSESSMENTS

In recent years emphasis has been removed from examinations. Instead, most States have phased in a system of **continuous assessments** which may or may not be supplemented by examinations. The problem lies in finding a way to compare students of all types of schools in competing for places in universities, colleges and technical courses to fit them for a career. Each State has a slightly different system; the crunch comes at the end of the first four years of secondary education, with the need for an examination or assessment which pupils can take with them into the workplace from age 15 or 16. Allocation of places in **tertiary education** courses from the age of 17 or 18, after completing two further optional years at secondary school, makes general academic assessment even more necessary. In NSW, for example, examinations have been phased out altogether: the schools provide a final 'aggregate' drawn from the pupil's performance in various subjects via continuous assessments. This is a trend around Australia, deemed fairer to pupils who may not respond well to do-or-die examinations and cramming.

EDUCATION IN ISOLATED AREAS

Apart from private schools, the only State-run institutions with facilities for school children living away from home are the **agricultural high schools** of New South Wales and Western Australia. There may be subsidies paid by a State government for transport costs in bringing children living far from the nearest school. However, some country schools in Western Australia and Tasmania have hostels attached to them for the benefit of those who would otherwise have to travel vast distances to school—or not go at all.

Australia has developed a novel system for bringing education to children with no access to boarding schools or hostels, and whose families prefer to have them live at home anyway. There are schools of the air, which link a teacher with a number of pupils studying at home via radio, as well as correspondence schools. Both government and private schools in isolated areas participate in such programmes; all schools in declared 'isolated' areas are expected to pool resources provided through government programmes to encourage participation and a higher standard of education for the children involved.

Correspondence lessons are usually supervised by a family member of the pupil studying at home. Lessons cater for pupils from primary age to matriculation. Each capital city in Australia has a correspondence school to administer the system. Video and audio tapes and electronic devices are distributed, helping to improve such services in recent years and the Loan Video Programme assists with video recorders, television monitors and videotaped education materials. Some States require payment of tuition fees in secondary school years.

Schools of the Air provide a radio classroom for children of the outback, and also need the participation and encouragement of a supervisor at home. Two-way radio equipment was first developed by the Flying Doctor Service for homes hundreds of kilometres apart in rural or desert Australia. Pupils and teacher talk directly to each other and satellite links as well as other advanced communications are being investigated for use in Schools of the Air.

LEAVING SCHOOL AND FINDING JOBS

Australia has a general school leaving age of 15, when a teenager can legally enter the workforce. However, a high level of youth unemployment stares first job-hunters in the face. Unemployment among Australians aged 16 to 25 was well over 20 per cent in the late 1980s, twice to four times the rate of most other developed countries and better only in comparison to youth employment prospects in Britain, Italy and France.

Yet Australian school-leavers are not breaking their necks to improve their education and chances of employment. The allures of the beach and 'dole' (unemployment benefits may be paid, see Chapter 13) are commonly blamed. On the other hand, the number of suitable jobs has shrunk with the economy. Successive State and Federal Governments have tried a variety of programmes and incentives in the past decade, to avoid the embarrassment of youth unemployment figures and the drain on the public purse. Employers and school-leavers are encouraged to find each other through training and apprenticeship schemes. Australia has one of the lowest rates of university entry, with only 20 per cent of school-leavers at matriculation level (aged 17 to 18) choosing to continue their education this way. But its facilities and opportunities for tertiary studies are among the best in the world.

TERTIARY EDUCATION

Australia has three kinds of tertiary education establishments:

- **Universities**, offering courses at undergraduate bachelor degree level, postgraduate diploma, master's degree and doctorate (PhD) standard
- **Colleges of Advanced Education** or **Institutes of Technology**, generally offering undergraduate associate diplomas, diplomas, bachelor degrees, postgraduate and master's degrees
- **Technical and Further Education (TAFE) Colleges,** and similar level institutions offering trade and technical courses, commercial and general studies to diploma level and, at some specific institutions, matriculation courses for people beyond the school system.

The States are responsible for tertiary education, but are reliant on the Federal Government for funding. Australian students are required to pay an **administration fee**, introduced in 1987 and set at $A250 a year at that time. This fee is waived for low income earners, who may have access to other financial help from the Government (see section later in this chapter).

As at schools, the academic year begins in late February and ends in December. The tertiary calendar is usually divided into **semesters**, broken by holidays which sometimes overlap with exam times. The main holiday period is in the summer months, from December to February. In Britain or America, students commonly leave their families to go to another city or State and have the experience of living away from home while furthering their education; but Australians usually attend a suitable course near their homes.

Overseas students who are *not* on scholarships or otherwise sponsored, are expected to contribute more fully to their tertiary education if they have approval to enter Australia as temporary residents to study (see Chapter 6).

UNIVERSITIES

Called 'unis' in Ausspeak, these take in some 200,000 new students each year. There are at least two universitites in every State and Territory, except for the Northern Territory which has none, and Tasmania, which has one...19 in all. Universities were first established in Sydney and Melbourne in the 1850s. Today many still tend to follow British or American traditions, and responsibility for academic matters is vested in university boards and committees. The more old-fashioned establishments are run by professorial boards, comprising professors, deans and heads of department. Members may be elected by their peers on the university academic staff.

Students play a role in university administration through **student unions**. Union fees (around $A200 a year in many places, at the time of writing) are part of the basic cost of university attendance, along with the administration fee and charges to people taking postgraduate or second degree courses. Books must also be bought by students, though secondhand bookshops on the campus or nearby may help reduce this expense.

The structure of courses varies, depending on the university and field of study. Generally, subjects like engineering, medicine and science require longer hours of lectures, tutorials or laboratory work than arts subjects and humanities, when students are expected to put more time into private research, reading and writing.

Assessment

Methods of assessing students' progress vary from university to university. Students are expected to attend tutorials, particularly, and it is not necessarily a disadvantage to express an opinion different from that of the lecturer or tutor. Continuous assessment, as in high school, is a trend for some courses and in some places this assessment is even made by the students themselves. But mid-year and final examinations are still standard at university to master's degree level in many fields.

All establishments offer research, master's and PhD programmes and a limited amount of coursework may be offered to complement a post-graduate research programme. However, award of a research degree is still based on the quality of a final thesis. Postgraduate diploma courses are usually shorter in duration and narrower in subject matter than master's courses.

Student life

University life on campus tends to revolve around bars, canteens and entertainments. Foreign students, often from South-East Asia or the Southern Pacific where Australia is keen to provide education as part of its international aid programme, are highly visible at universities around Australia. They, too, often have their own social clubs alongside other minority ethnic, religious and political groups whch thrive and mix in the hothouse university environment.

Most campuses have **student counselling services** to help students meet the requirements of university life, while lecturers and tutors are expected to be available to advise on problems relating to studies.

Universities provide **housing** for eligible students, usually those from remote areas or overseas, in rooms on campus or near the university. However, it is not usual for university students to go to another city to study, as in Europe or America, and most city-based undergraduates remain in the family home.

In all universities, teaching and research are inseparable. Academic staff are selected through world-wide advertisements and universities enjoy rare freedom in Australia to recruit from abroad and so obtain temporary entry permits for foreign academics, in order to improve local education standards.

COLLEGES OF ADVANCED EDUCATION, TAFE AND RE-EDUCATING ADULTS

The advanced education sector was established in the 1960s as an alternative to the academic traditions of university, with 47 such colleges being established and catering to 175,000 students by the late 1980s. **Technical and Further Education** (TAFE) colleges run both vocational (job-oriented) and non-vocational courses. Like most universities which offer opportunities to people who finished schooldays long ago, these colleges are geared for adult education as well as the needs of school-leavers preparing for an initial career. High unemployment and changing technology has accelerated demand from adults wanting to retrain or gain additional expertise.

As in many countries, Australians can expect to have not just one career during their working lives, as technologies and demand for goods and services change. Apart from the government tertiary sector, there are a number of **voluntary bodies** which also provide a chance for adults to retrain. The Workers' Educational Association in New South Wales and South Australia, for example, caters for subjects from philosophy to television scriptwriting, as well as courses for trade unionists. Young Men's Christian Associations and Young Women's Christian Associations also offer a range of non-vocational studies for adults while the opportunity for non-degree studies at **Universities of the Third Age**, has taken off among older, retired people wanting to learn for pleasure.

The TAFE colleges offer matriculation preparation for people who may not have finished high school, or who want to sit their finals again in order to gain entry to a specific tertiary course. Migrants are offered English-language studies. Correspondence courses are available to students who live too far from a TAFE or higher education college to attend full or part-time classes.

Colleges of advanced education (CAE)

Colleges of advanced education include a range of facilities such as:

- large technical institutions in the capital cities
- non-technological, multi-purpose institutions providing higher education opportunities in metropolitan areas, with teacher education as a main activity
- multi-purpose colleges providing higher education opportunities in non-metropolitan areas
- specialist institutions in the arts, agriculture, allied health and maritime studies

Colleges of advanced education cover a wide range of fields including teacher education, engineering, nursing, art and design, architecture, building, business studies, social welfare, music, law, journalism, librarianship, surveying and pharmacy. This sector of government-funded education is intended for people who have completed full secondary school studies and CAEs have broader entry requirements than universities. They are also more flexible in terms of part-time courses. Students aim to attain a diploma, degree or postgraduate diploma award. Qualifications from such colleges are often regarded as being on a par with a university degree, though with not quite the prestige of a comparable course — if any — available at a university.

Technical and Further Education (TAFE)

Technical and Further Education colleges provide tertiary education at sub-trade, trade and technical level. Some states, like Victoria, have a well-developed TAFE support system at secondary school level, the so-called 'technical schools'. Such schools offering relevant subjects provide an education base in certain skills which could be needed in vocational studies at a TAFE college.

Throughout Australia, TAFE courses are used to supplement apprenticeships or on-the-job training. They provide theoretical or practical back-up on a part-time basis, in combination with the paid apprenticeship or job. Many people wishing to become skilled tradesmen (often very well paid jobs in Australia) leave high school about Year 4 (aged 15 or 16) to begin TAFE studies. Others complete the full six years at high school before starting the trade course, culminating in an award or certificate.

FINANCIAL ASSISTANCE TO AUSTRALIAN STUDENTS

The Federal Government has various schemes of grants, loans and payments for students at postgraduate, tertiary and secondary levels;

these are administered through the Department of Education and Youth Affairs in Canberra.

- The **Postgraduate Awards Scheme** (PAS) is administered under rules which give assistance on a competitive basis for higher education degree studies (master's and doctorates) at universities and colleges of advanced education. The benefits include living away from home allowances and dependants' allowances which are not means-tested, though they are taxable if total assessable income exceeds certain limits. Travel expenses and establishment allowances may also be granted to eligible high achievers on low incomes.

- The **Tertiary Education Assistance Scheme** (TEAS) is the main student funding programme at undergraduate level, and provides living allowances to full-time students enrolled at approved courses at universities, colleges of advances education and colleges of technical and further education. Students at private (non-government) institutions, like secretarial courses or business colleges, may also be approved for TEAS. Other TEAS benefits include an incidental allowance to pay student fees, dependants' allowances and assistance with travel costs.

Adult or mature students returning to full-time studies covering the final year of secondary schooling (because they want to gain entry to university or some other tertiary course) may be eligible to benefits comparable to TEAS, under the **Adult Secondary Education Assistance Scheme.** The **Secondary Allowances Scheme** will pay low income parents a subsidy for children attending the final two years at high school, prior to matriculation or further education. The **Assistance for Isolated Children Scheme** gives financial help to parents of children who cannot attend school due to distance, physical or intellectual disabilities, who must study by correspondence or live at a second home or hostel to make it possible for them to attend school.

15
Taking It All With You

So you've gained permission to live and work in Australia. Now you want to know: can I take it all with me?

If your 'all' features Aunty Mabel's home-made jams, a muddy lawnmower or your pet llama, the answer is probably 'no'. But a very clean family car, dogs and cats, or even your private airship will probably meet with a conditional 'yes'. For Australian red tape on customs and imports covers practically everything and should give you much to think about well before you start packing. Will it be worth taking things along at all if, in the long run, they'll be less trouble to replace in Australia?

Customs

Furthermore, the customs rules are in a state of flux. Since 1985, the Federal Government has been mulling over changes suggested in the *Report on Passenger Concessions*, compiled by the Industries' Assistance Commission. The IAC advises Canberra's lawmakers on how to help the local economy with import restrictions, taxes and suchlike. So the tax-free allowances to people bringing cars, refrigerators, even sailing boats with them to Australia as permanent settlers could be affected. At the time of writing, the Government had still not made a decision on any changes — though it would be wise to check with the **Collector of Customs** in the Australian port or airport where your goods are to arrive, to discover the latest interpretation of the rules and regulations. Or write to

● The Controller-General, Australian Customs Service, Barton, ACT 2600 and/or the Australian Embassy or High Commission near you.

Hygiene and quarantine

Apart from certain taxes and customs charges which may apply to your possessions, rules are enforced to prevent unauthorised animal and plant

life migrating with you. In case you unwittingly carry microscopic
beasties on your person, you will be sprayed on disembarkation at an
Australian airport...but that's just the start. Wouldn't it be awful to send
an old lawnmower and gardening tools Down Under — only to find they
must be stored in quarantine for months, fumigated, cleaned, and all the
bills charged to you — along with whatever you forked out for shipping
in the first place? Australians are especially concerned to enforce strict
rules to keep their continent free of the foreign diseases and pests which
could be a health risk or damage its important agricultural base. Strict
quarantine and fumigation procedures apply to all pets, cars, business or
household goods you may want to take to Australia with you.

Do *not* sell up and ship out before you have *absolute approval* from
federal immigration authorities. A State Government office in London
recently led a would-be immigrant to believe he was sure to win a
migration visa on the strength of a job offered by that same State
Government. The unfortunate man sold his house, his car, packed for
the big move—only to find the Federal seal had *not* been given to the
application. Immigration officials enforced a rule that 'his' job had to be
advertised in Australia — and when it was, someone already living there
was deemed suitable.

RESTRICTED AND PROHIBITED IMPORTS

First and foremost, you should note those goods which cannot be taken
into Australia at all, unless special clearance is obtained:

- **narcotic drugs,** including drugs of dependence of many kinds like
  barbiturates, amphetamines, hallucinogens and tranquillisers
  which must be cleared at customs when you enter. The maximum
  penalty, if found guilty of trying to illegally import such
  substances, is 25 years' imprisonment and/or a fine of $A100,000
  (at time of writing) if traffickable quantities are involved.

- **firearms and weapons.** Taking certain types of weapons into
  Australia is strictly policed and approval must be given if you plan
  to do so. Guns such as air, gas, flare, spearguns and starting
  pistols must be declared at customs. Importation of spring-bladed
  knives, daggers, swordsticks and knuckledusters are prohibited.

QUARANTINE

Australia is free of many of the world's worst animal and vegetable pests
and diseases, and is justifiably rather paranoid about keeping things this
way. When making your **customs declaration** you must draw attention to

anything you plan to take with you which could possibly contain or carry pests or disease. Commonly, foodstuffs like preserves or favourite delicacies from another country are confiscated if detected, and people suspected of knowingly trying to sneak Aunty Mabel's apple jelly through customs end up in the Federal Court. You are required to sign a declaration saying you have no such items in your luggage, before you enter Australia as a tourist or resident. If you want exemption for the type of goods which fall into the categories listed below, a permit from the Australian Quarantine Service is necessary.

Prohibited items

Though the rules may change with the scientific evidence, items prohibited at the time of writing or subject to quarantine include:

- **food** of any kind, including tinned or packaged goods
- **plants** or parts of plants, living or dead, including fruits, nuts, wood, bamboo, straw or objects made of plant materials. In planning the furniture or household effects you want to take to Australia with you, as well as when having these packed for removal, be sure to select any wooden items carefully. If they are found to be infested with borers or contain other insects, the quarantine officials may demand they be fumigated at your expense before they are allowed to join you in your new home.
- **animals** or parts of animals, dead or alive, stuffed or mounted
- **animal products** like feathers, hairs, skins, shells and hatching eggs or items manufactured from wildlife endangered or otherwise, such as lizards, snakes, crocodiles, whales, elephants, zebras, rhinoceroses or members of the cat family. People both coming to and leaving Australia should be aware that articles of clothing, shoes, handbags, trophies, ornaments or anything else made from a protected species of wildlife may be seized under Federal law. If you plan to take such things to Australia, an **import permit** must be obtained in advance. Australian authorities will only accept such items on production of an export permit from the relevant wildlife authority of the country where the restricted animal product originated.
- **equipment,** such as saddles, used with horses or other animals
- **biological specimens**, including vaccines, cultures and blood
- **soil**
- **motor vehicles,** caravans and trailers which must be inspected on arrival by quarantine officers who may request they be steamcleaned at the importer's expense, if found to contain animal, plant or soil traces.

Dogs and cats

Dogs and cats can only be brought to Australia from **approved countries**, and must spend at least 60 days in quarantine at special facilities in Sydney, Melbourne and Brisbane in Australia. However, your pet may first have to spend time in and out of quarantine in another country en route. It all depends where your pet comes from. The rules are tailored to prevent the transfer of particular diseases which exist in the country or continent of an animal's origin and may be complicated. Dogs and cats from Britain and Ireland must spend 60 days in quarantine in Australia. Those from prescribed countries in the Pacific region must spend 4 months in quarantine and, if from other approved countries, 9 months' quarantine may be required. Furthermore, Australia stipulates that the pets can only enter Australia after 30 days' residence in Britain or Hawaii, which have their own quarantine rules. If from continental Europe, for instance, your pet must enter Australia via Britain — and Britain imposes its own six month additional quarantine period due to the threat of rabies. Then the animal must spend 30 days *out* of quarantine before being transported and again quarantined in Australia.

So think carefully about whether it is worth imposing months of isolation from their familiar people and places on your pets. A permit to import must also be obtained before bringing your animal into Australia.

Birds

However, if you are thinking of taking your beloved canary — or any other feathered friend—don't. Though there are plans to build a bird quarantine centre in South Australia for the import of birds for commercial purposes, at the time of writing *all* birds and associated items (like eggs) were prohibited. Indeed, they face certain death if discovered on arrival. Likewise, any animal for which an import permit has *not* been obtained will be destroyed on arrival.

Quarantine information

Australia's quarantine rules alter with time, according to the latest scientific evidence. For the latest quarantine information and the rules as they apply to animals from your country of origin, contact:

The Director of Quarantine
The Australian Quarantine and Inspection Service
Department of Primary Industry
Edmund Barton Building
Canberra 2600, Australia

Or contact Australia's regional veterinary authority on quarantine via the local High Commission or Embassy.

DUTIES AND TAXES

Everything you hope to bring to Australia as a tourist, temporary visitor or as an immigrant is subject to customs evaluation and possibly

- import duty
- excise and/or
- Australian sales taxes

It makes no difference whether the goods are accompanied or unaccompanied baggage.

However there are many concessions — especially for people coming to live permanently — dealt with later in this Chapter. Occasionally changes are made to the tax calculations and exemptions applied to people importing items for commercial or personal use. For full current details of the customs rules as they may apply to your special circumstances, contact the authorities suggested at the start of this Chapter. As a rule, no exemptions apply to the following items, on which excise or import duty will be imposed, apart from some exemptions on quantities:

- **alcoholic liquor**. This is subject to the current rate of duty if arriving unaccompanied. However, anyone over the age of 18 entering Australia with up to 1 litre of alcoholic liquor, including wine and beer, can bring this in duty free;

- **tobacco, cigarettes, cigars**. As above, unaccompanied goods of this kind are subject to the current rate of import duty. People over the age of 18 arriving with up to 200 cigarettes or 250 grams of cigars or 250 grams of tobacco may bring these through customs duty free;

- **articles purchased outside Australia** being imported on behalf of people resident in Australia. These are subject to import duties and taxes;

- **articles that a person outside Australia** has asked you to take to a person in Australia. These are subject to import duties and taxes;

- goods sent as **freight**, and goods sent directly to Australia from shops on your behalf would also be subject to regular import duties and taxes.

Exemptions on personal effects

'Personal effects' (ie the things you take in your own luggage) are duty free providing they:

- are your own property
- arrive on the same aircraft or ship on which you travel
- are suitable and intended for your own use
- are not intended for 'commercial purposes' (sale, rent, hire, etc)
- are not imported in commercial quantities

Duty free personal effects are, in the jargon of Australian customs authorities, 'articles of the type normally carried on your person or in your personal baggage including jewellery and toilet requisites, wristwatch, cigarette lighter etc but not electrical entertainment appliances (stereos, cassettes, walkmans and so forth), binoculars, portable typewriters, exposed films of your travels, photographic cameras, still or movie cameras, personal sporting requisites including sporting and camping equipment of travelling sportsmen'.

Clothing also rates a mention, though it is worth remembering that furs valued at more than a certain amount ($A150 at the time of writing) or which have not been owned and used by you for at least 12 months *are* dutiable.

General duty-free concessions apply only to people coming to Australia to take up residence for the first time. These concessions apply to items defined as gifts, souvenirs, articles unused or less than 12 months old and other normally dutiable items as long as each passenger has not more than $A200 (at time of writing) worth of these. Items exceeding the stipulated value but bringing the total to less than $A360 (at time of writing) per person, must have a 20 per cent duty paid on their excess value. The authorities allow family groups, including children under the age of 10, to club together to make the most of the concessions applying to individuals. But of course people under 18 cannot claim the concessionary rate or exemptions on cigarettes, tobacco or alcohol declared as their 'share'. Furthermore, the concessions for travellers under 18 is half the adult rate: that is, the first $A100 free (at time of writing), the next $A80 at 20 per cent duty, and full duty or sales tax on eligible items thereafter.

People who object to the customs charges made on their belongings can only appeal to the senior customs officer stationed at the port or airport of arrival.

Exemptions — unaccompanied luggage

There are certain items which can come into Australia as unaccompanied luggage which are duty free. The most generous concessions apply to belongings of people coming to make their homes in the country. All these things fall within the personal and general concession categories applying to immigrants coming to Australia for the first time:

- furniture or household goods which the importer or importer's family have owned and used for 12 months prior to departure for Australia
- goods on which sales tax has previously been paid in Australia which are being sent back there
- fur clothing that the owner and importer has used for at least 12 months before departure
- non-motorised bicycles and motorcycles without sidecars
- motor vehicles, caravans, and boats subject to conditions given later in this Chapter
- plant, equipment or machinery subject to conditions given later

But remember that unaccompanied items must fulfil exactly the same conditions, including prohibited items, quarantine and hygiene, as the things coming into the country with the visitor or immigrant.

Commercial equipment — special exemptions for immigrants

Secondhand machinery, plant and equipment which you may want to take to Australia for use in your job or business is allowed in duty free if:

- you have come to Australia for the first time to take up permanent residence immediately
- the goods are the importer's personal property and you have personally owned and used these goods overseas for the entire 12 months before coming to Australia. Naturally, it is best to produce receipts, examples of your work, or other proof to show customs officers in case they ask for evidence
- you will be in a position to put these items to your own use. For example, people given a visa on the basis they will be retiring from business activities in Australia and yet applying to bring in factory machinery, could meet a coolish reception from the customs officer
- you can convince the customs authorities that you will be using the goods for the purposes they are intended
- during the first two years in Australia the items are not sold, hired, mortgaged or otherwise disposed of. The two-year period specified begins from the time you start using the equipment for their intended commercial purpose.

However, if machinery, plant or equipment is owned by a company or partnership, or if the individual owner is not over 18 years old, duty must be paid at the regular rate.

Also, some types of machinery in this category are subject to licencing controls in Australia, so it is advisable to check with customs authorities in the State or Territory where you plan to import, before taking the trouble and expense to transport them Down Under.

Exemptions — motor vehicles

A person coming to Australia as an immigrant is allowed to import one motor vehicle duty free. Taxes on imported vehicles are generally high, making many models—considered quite ordinary abroad—expensive and exotic in Australia. In the past large profits have been made by immigrants and, more often, returning Australian travellers, bringing in foreign cars duty free and selling them on arrival. Now there are strict rules to stop abuse of this concession, and it is possible these will be further tightened to protect the interests of licensed car dealers and importers. Before you decide if it is worth transporting your car, truck, or other motor vehicle to Australia, it is wise to consider whether it:

- conforms with Australian **design rule requirements,** as enforced by the motor registration authorities in the State or Territory where you will be living. If in doubt, check with the State or Territory Government or your present motoring organisation, if it has contacts in Australia. Necessary safety features which must be fitted to all cars driven in Australia include seat belts and head restraints on front seats.

- meets other **registration requirements** of the State or Territory where you plan to live, again through the particular Government or a motoring organisation.

Together with customs and shipping charges, it was estimated in 1987 it would cost more than £1,000 to transport a car from Britain to Australia. Wherever the vehicle comes from, and whatever its condition on departure, you could be charged for steamcleaning, quarantine inspection, wharfage and storage in Australia—as well as delivery charges to take it from the docks to prepare for driving in Australia. If the car exceeds the high valuation threshold applied by customs authorities in assessing sales taxes and duties (see below), that expense will be even greater.

Import conditions on motor vehicles taken into Australia by migrants

Vehicles may be imported to Australia duty free and exempt of sales tax by persons over the age of 18 who prove to customs authorities they are

Shipping your vehicle — other considerations

1. If the vehicle is **left-hand drive**, what would be the cost and viability of converting it to right-hand drive, as necessary under Australian regulations?

2. **Shipping charges**, including after-arrival handling charges and clearances.

3. The **cost of similar new vehicles** in Australia. Again, you may discover this through a motoring organisation in Australia or in your present home, via State or Territory Government motor transport authorities, or simply by perusing the new and used car sales advertisements of Australian newspapers at reading rooms in the nearest embassy or high commission, or at a State Government office abroad.

4. Whether **spare parts and repairs** to your vehicle would be readily available in Australia. Again, this is information available through motoring organisations and could tip the balance in favour of buying a car there. Refer Chapter 11 **Driving in Australia**, for more details.

5. **How long will it take** before the vehicle joins you in Australia, if it is to arrive after you do?

6. If the car is to arrive before you, the amount of **customs surety** you will be obliged to pay (sometimes the entire value of the vehicle — see the guidelines below) before it can be released to you.

Consider the age and condition of the vehicle generally in the light of the points made above about conforming to design and registration regulations and Australian road conditions mentioned in the Chapter on **Driving in Australia.**

going to take up permanent residence (an immigrant's visa would be sufficient). The vehicle must have been personally owned and used by the importer for six continuous calendar months (or 184 continuous days) prior to departure for Australia. Company-owned vehicles do not qualify for this customs concession. Only one vehicle per adult migrant is allowed under these rules.

In some cases, a security with **financial surety** must be given to customs, to help convince them that the car is for the immigrant's personal use in Australia for 12 calendar months. Vehicles five years old or less require a surety of 90 per cent of the customs value. For vehicles over five years old, the rate is 57.5 per cent. The surety may be in cash, Australian Commonwealth Bonds, or a guarantee document issued by an approved institution, such as a bank. The type of surety required will be decided by Australian customs authorities. It will be refunded or cancelled provided the vehicle has *not* been disposed of within 12 months of importation, so there is still some room for an immigrant to make a healthy profit if and when it is sold.

The period of ownership and use is calculated from the date the migrant registers his or her vehicle, or from the time it is delivered to the owner for driving before going to Australia, whichever is later — up to the date the person leaves for Australia or when the vehicle is delivered there, whichever is earlier.

By 'used', the customs authorities mean the vehicle must have been continually used by the intending migrant or his/her family in each country in which they and the vehicle have been located.

By 'family', the customs authorities generally mean a husband and wife and their children aged less than 18 years.

EXTRA CARS, NEW CARS, TEMPORARY RESIDENTS, VISITORS AND TOURISTS

Sales tax and import duties must be paid by:

- people who cannot convince customs authorities they are coming to Australia to take up permanent residence
- people whose car is too new
- people who exceed the allowance of one vehicle per adult or are otherwise rejected for concessions

However, tourists or short-term residents/visitors obtaining a **Carnet** or similar document through their motoring organisation in their home country may bring suitable vehicles into Australia and avoid these charges. Arrangements must be made with an Australian motoring organisation to guarantee the removal of the vehicle at the end of the visit; financial surety may be required by the customs authorities, refundable if they are satisfied the vehicle has left Australia. Carnets are generally valid for up to one year.

FURNITURE AND HOUSEHOLD EFFECTS

As an immigrant, furniture and household items which you and/or your family have owned and used for 12 months or more preceding departure for Australia will be admitted free of duty, whether they accompany you on arrival or not. These items include:

- household appliances such as washing machines, refrigerators etc
- household linen, blankets, bedding, quilts etc

- chinaware, glassware, silverware, cutlery, household utensils and ornaments
- furniture including pianos, stereos, radios, television sets, projectors etc.

TEMPORARY RESIDENTS AND VISITORS

You should be able to take the things you need during your stay free of import charges if going to Australia for a temporary job posting, as an overseas student, working holidaymaker or other purpose. But you must satisfy customs officials that any household or other items are for your *personal* use, not for sale etc. These items must also comply with rules on quarantine, hygiene and not be otherwise outlawed.

You will be asked to sign an **undertaking to remove** such items again within 12 months or longer, depending on your visa and any extensions you get to it. However, a **financial guarantee** — cash or documentary — may be necessary as a surety. This is based on the sales taxes and/or import duties which apply to the goods you want to take with you to Australia. If customs officials decide you or the goods do not qualify for any concessions, the normal sales taxes and/or import duty will be charged.

ELECTRICAL APPLIANCES — AUSTRALIAN STANDARDS

It may not be worth the trouble and expense to take electrical equipment and household appliances to Australia. Apart from the size and weight of such goods, consider whether they conform with the standard Australian electricity supply, at 240 volts AC (50 hertz). If not, they may be dangerous or impossible to use. If modified, they may be explosive.

For **colour television** the Australian standard is 625 line PAL. But even sets designed for PAL may need modifications to receive television broadcasts in Australia. If in doubt, check with electrical retailers and authorities before you leave and, on arrival, have appliances checked by local electricity (or gas) authorities before you use them.

Oz-speak

AN INTRODUCTION TO AUSTRALIAN SLANG

apples — as in: "She'll be apples, mate." Everything will be OK.

arvo — afternoon.

award — as in: "The Australian Arbitration Commission yesterday increased the award for left-legged firemen by 2.25 per cent..." Refers to the wages and conditions awarded to workers in particular industries.

billy — tin pot used for boiling water, tea or cooking on a camp fire.

blue — as in "'aving a blue with the missus." Could mean a row, an argument, a tiff, even physical violence. See **domestic** below.

bust a gut — as in: "Don't bust a gut over your tax bill." Reference to the deleterious effects of worry or hard work.

bombo, plonk — cheap wine.

Bruce — could be your given name, but a bit of a cliché since Jasons and Julians and Simons also abound in Australia, as in other Anglo societies.

Brucellosis — a disease which infects cattle and even humans, not to be confused with Brucelene or Brucette, which is what sheilas are supposed to be named when they are not Cheryl, Dorreen or Raelene — though once again there is no shortage of Sarahs, Amys and Emilies Down Under.

corroboree — originally an Aboriginal assembly, now a reference to any large and noisy gathering.

dead set — an oath, a promise, as in "Strewth, mate, 'course I'll see youse down the pub this arvo...DEAD SET!"

digger — a soldier, though before that a term for a worker in the gold rush era in New South Wales and Victoria of the 19th century. Now used with 'mate' or 'cobber', the word has been associated with Australian-born media magnate Rupert Murdoch, who was dubbed the 'Dirty Digger' by his competitors in Fleet Street in reference to the

style of tabloid journalism he popularised in Britain's snooty
newspaper world.

dinkum — as in fair dinkum, dinky-di. Something true-blue Australian.

domestic — as in 'having a domestic'. Can mean a very bad 'blue' (see
above). Police jargon for a family argument serious enough for them
to be called to the scene, in response to neighbours' complaints or
because at least one party has become uncontrollably violent.

esky — usually a plastic box for keeping drinks cold in; otherwise known
as a chillybin.

Fremantle Doctor — the sea breeze off Perth. Fremantle is the Western
Australian capital's port town.

**frosty, tinny, tube, amber fluid or nectar, neck oil, singing syrup,
brewery broth,** etc — beer.

jumbuck — aboriginal word for sheep (of which there are more
than 130 million in Australia).

lemonhead, surfie — someone who enjoys surf board riding for sport
and the beach as a social centre.

mate — sometimes applied to a sheila. Unlike other English-speaking
societies in which a male person will use 'mate' only when talking to
another man (especially if unsure of the other's given name), women in
Australia commonly find themselves being referred to as 'mate' by a
bloke. Note the reverse does not apply. A woman would not refer to a
man as a 'sheila'.

matilda — swagman's swag or pack which he 'waltzes' round the
outback.

prawn — shrimp, shellfish.

on — favourite Australian preposition, as in to 'go ON the grog' (start
an alcoholic binge); 'go ON the wagon' (give up alcohol); to 'carry
ON', 'rave ON', etc.

Pom or **Pommy** — a Brit or Briton. First noted in Australian usage
around 1912 in association with immigrants from England arriving
under schemes for assisted passage to the fledgling nation. Theorists
say 'Pom' could be an acronym of Prisoner Of Mother England
(POME) or a reference to pomegranate, and the similarly red, no
doubt sunburnt cheeks of the British arrivals.

raw prawn — deception, a joke: as in, "Don't come the raw prawn
with me, mate."

rubbidy — watering hole, pub, bar, club, hotel...anywhere refreshments
with the frothy, icy, alcoholic qualities of beer and ever-more popular
wine are available.

Strine — abbreviation of 'orstralian' referring to the language.

stroppy — annoyed, irritated.

uey, lefty, righty — driving terminology, as in an instruction to the person behind the wheel to 'chuck a lefty, mate...', advising you to turn left. 'Uey' (rhyming with 'dewy') refers to a U-turn.

rat face — as the metaphoric usage of 'veggie' below, referring to someone who is incapable after too much of a good (or bad) thing.

pressy — present, gift. In fact, Oz-speak features the suffix -ie, -y, -i being applied to objects and names. Other examples include Aussie, lolly (sweet, candy or money), undies (see below) and people's surnames, as in **Hawkie**, a well known 'polly' (politician) and sometime Prime Minister of Australia.

Reg Grundies — Reginald's Undies — underwear. An example of the Australian addiction to rhyming slang. Reg Grundy was a television producer who came to prominence Down Under in the 1960s and 70s. His name lives on in international television production, as well as in this convenient euphemism for bras, vests, slips, singlets and underpants.

rort — something of a con trick, a method of making easy and probably illegal money. It also has political connotations. The *Sydney Morning Herald* described rort in 1981 as 'a charmingly flexible term to cover such practices as stacking branch membership, rigging elections, cooking branch records, as a last resort, losing all branch records to frustrate a head office inquiry.'

sheila — dinky di person of the female persuasion. References to sheilas — not to mention some of the other more derogatory slang terms for things and people which do not happen to be blokes, guys and fellas, can make strong feminists weep. Read Germaine Greer if you insist on knowing more...

shout — to buy a round of drinks at the pub. "Wouldn't shout if a shark bit ya!" — expression denoting disgust at a person's failure to buy a mate a beer.

vegemite — yeast extract sandwich or biscuit spread. Tastes black, salty and like marmite.

veggie — could be a literal reference to vegetables or, metaphorically, to a person's mental and physical condition after heavy drinking or drug-taking, for instance.

yabby — a freshwater crayfish. Also reference to a wicket keeper in cricket.

yakka — work, as in 'lotsa hard yakka'.

Further Reading

General

Brown, Harry. *Retiring Abroad?* Northcote House 1987. 288pp.
Brown, Harry. *Working Abroad?* Northcote House 1986. 160pp.
Fairley, Alan. *The Observer's Book of National Parks of Australia.* Warne 1981.
Mead, Robin. *Australia.* Batsford 1983. 173pp.
Notes for Newcomers: Australia. Women's Corona Society.
Peterson, Vicki. *Australia.* Cassell 1980. 186pp.
Sherington, Geoffrey. *Australia's Immigrants 1788-1978.* Allen & Unwin 1980.
Sharpless, Reginald. *Pommy in the Outback.* New Horizon 1982. 190pp.
Wheeler, Tony. *Australia: Travel Survival Kit.* Lonely Planet 1983. 576pp.

Background and social life

Campion, Edmund. *Rockhoppers: Growing Up Catholic in Australia.* Penguin 1982.
Carter, Paul. *The Road to Botany Bay: Australian Civilisation to 1986.* Faber 1987. 300pp.
Chapple, S G. *The Ramblings of an Australian.* Stockwell 1981. 58pp.
Grant, Bruce. *The Australian Dilemma: A New Kind of Western Society.* Macdonald Futura 1983. 320pp.
Hansen, Gary. *Australia: Impressions of a Continent.* Angus & Robertson 1978.
Horne, Donald. *The Lucky Country: Australia in the Sixties.* Angus & Robertson 1978.
Keneally, Thomas. *The Outback.* Hodder & Stoughton 1983. 256pp.
McGregor, Craig. *The Australian People.* Hodder & Stoughton 1980. 334pp.
McLean, Hazel. *Ladies One Side, Gentlemen the Other.* Carolina 1987. 150pp.
    (Australian social life 1920 to 1950)
Moore, David & Hall, Rodney. *Australia: Image of a Nation 1850-1950.* Collins 1983. 335pp.
Tomlinson, Gerry (Ed). *Bring Plenty of Pickles: Letters from an Emigrant Family 1842-1902.* Tomlinson 1986. 80pp.
Terrill, Ross. *The Australians: A Journey to the Heart of a Nation.* Bantam 1987.

The Australian economy

Cost of Living & Housing Survey. Commonwealth Bank of Australia. 42pp.
Establishing a New Business in Australia: The Legal Implications. Ellison, Hewison & Whitehead, London 1985. 26pp
Gruen, F H. *Surveys of Australian Economies.* Allen & Unwin 1979. 266pp.
Head, Brian. *Politics and Development.* Allen & Unwin 1986. 280pp.
Head, Brian. *State and Economy in Australia.* Oxford University Press 1983.
Kamm, Herbert & Pepper, Thomas. *Will She Be Right? The Future of Australia.* University of Queensland Press 1980. 199pp.
Martin, Joseph. *The Management of the Australian Economy.* University of Queensland Press 1979. 237pp.
Wealth, Poverty & Survival. Allen & Unwin 1983. 240pp.
Whitwell, Greg. *The Treasury Line.* Allen & Unwin 1986. 320pp.

Useful Addresses and Contacts

AUSTRALIAN GOVERNMENT REPRESENTATIVES

United Kingdom

Agent-General for New South Wales, New South Wales House, 66 Strand, London WC2N 5LZ. Tel: 01-839 6651

Agent-General for Queensland, Queensland House, 392-393 Strand, London WC2R 0LZ. Tel: 01-836 3224

Agent-General & Trade Commissioner for South Australia, South Australia House, 50 Strand, London WC2N 5LW. Tel: 01-930 7471

Agent-General for Victoria, Victoria House, Melbourne Place, Strand, London WC2B 4LG. Tel: 01-836 2656

Agent-General for Western Australia, Western Australia House, 115-116 Strand, London WC2R 0AJ. Tel: 01-240 2881

Australian Consulate, 80 Hanover Street, Edinburgh EH2 2HQ. Tel: 031-226 6271

Australian Consulate, Chatsworth House, Lever Street, Manchester M1 2DL. Tel: 061-228 1344

Australian High Commission, Australia House, Strand, London WC2B 4LA. Tel: 01-379 4334

Australian Trade Commission (AUSTRADE), Australia House, Strand, London WC2B 4LA. Tel: 01-379 4334

The Registrar, Department of Social Security, Australia House, Strand, London WC2B 4LA.

Migration & Visa Enquiries, Australia House, Strand, London WC2B 4LA. Tel: 01-836 7123

Key areas overseas

Australian Embassy, 15 Messogeion Street, Ambelokipi 11526 (Box 3070), Athens, Greece.

Australian Consulate-General, Harbour Centre, 25 Harbour Road (PO Box 820 Central), Wanchai, Hong Kong.

Australian Embassy, Fitzwilton House, Wilton Terrace, Dublin 2, Ireland.

Australian Embassy, Via Alessandria 215, Rome 00198, Italy.

Australian High Commission, Development House, Moi Avenue (PO Box 30360), Nairobi, Kenya.

Australian High Commission, 6 Jalan Yap Kwan Seng, Kuala Lumpur, Malaysia.

Australian High Commission, 25 Napier Road (Tanglin Post Office, PO Box 470), Singapore 10.

Australian Embassy, Mutual & Federal Building, 220 Vermeulen Street, Pretoria 0001, South Africa.

Australian Embassy, 1601 Massachusetts Avenue NW, Washington DC 20036, USA.

USEFUL CONTACTS IN THE UNITED KINGDOM

Australian Airlines, 7 Swallow Street, London W1. Tel: 01-434 3864
Australian British Chamber of Commerce, 615 Linen Hall, Regent Street, London W1.
  Tel: 01-439 0086
Australian Broadcasting Corporation, 54 Portland Place, London W1. Tel: 01-631 4456
Australian Financial & Migrant Information Service, Commonwealth Bank of Australia,
  Aldwych House, Aldwych, London WC2. Tel: 01-242 4488
Australian Forwarding Agency Ltd, 44 Aldwych, London WC2. Tel: 01-460 8535
Australian Housing & Travel, 28 Melbourne Place, London WC2. Tel: 01-836 4016
Australian & New Zealand Banking Group, 55 Gracechurch Street, London EC3. Tel:
  01-280 3100
Australian Removal Services, 147 Masons Hill, Bromley, Kent. Tel: 01-460 8535
Australian Reunion & Holiday Club, 200 Buckingham Palace Road, London SW1.
  Tel: 01-821 4108
Australian Studies Centre, 27 Russell Square, London WC1. Tel: 01-580 5876
Australian Tourist Commission, Heathcote House, 20 Saville Row, London W1X 1AE.
  Tel: 01-434 4371
Australian Union of Students Student Travel (UK) Ltd, 117 Euston Road, London
  NW1. Tel: 01-388 2261
Commonwealth Institute, Kensington High Street, London W8. Tel: 01-603 4535
Department of Health & Social Security, Overseas Branch, Benton Park Road,
  Newcastle upon Tyne NE98 1YX. Tel: 0632-857111
Flinders Australian Bookshop, 45 Burton Street, London WC1. Tel: 01-388 6080
Professional & Executive Recruitment Overseas, 4-5 Grosvenor Place, London
  SW1X 7SB. Tel: 01-235 9985
Qantas Airways Ltd, Qantas House, 395 King Street, London W6. Tel: 01-748 3181
Westpac Banking Corporation (formerly the Bank of New South Wales), Walbrook
  House, Walbrook, London EC4. Tel: 01-626 4500
Women's Corona Society, Room 501, Eland House, Stag Place, London SW1E 5DH.
  Tel: 01-828 1652
World-wide Education Service, Strode House, 44-50 Osnaburgh Street, London
  NW1 3NN. Tel: 01-387 9228

USEFUL CONTACTS IN AUSTRALIA

Customs offices

The Secretary, Department of Industry & Commerce, Canberra, ACT 2600. Tel: 062-72
  3944
The Collector of Customs, Sydney, NSW 2000. Tel: 02-2 0521
The Collector of Customs, Darwin, NT 5790. Tel: 089-81 4444
The Collector of Customs, Brisbane, Queensland 4000. Tel: 07-227 0444
The Collector of Customs, Port Adelaide, SA 5015. Tel: 08-47 9211
The Collector of Customs, Hobart, Tasmania 7000. Tel: 002-30 1201
The Collector of Customs, Melbourne, Victoria 3000. Tel: 03-61 11555
The Collector of Customs, Fremantle, WA 6160. Tel: 09-336 0222

Motoring organisations

National Roads & Motorists' Association (NRMA), 92-96 Northbourne Avenue,
  Canberra City, ACT 2601. Tel: 062-43 8888

National Roads & Motorists' Association (NRMA), 151 Clarence Street, Sydney, NSW 2000. Tel: 02-260 9222

Automobile Association of Northern Territory, 79-81 Smith Street, Darwin, NT 5790. Tel: 089-81 3837

Royal Automobile Club of Queensland, 300 St Paul's Terrace, Fortitude Valley, Brisbane, Queensland 4006. Tel: 07-253 2444

Royal Automobile Association of South Australia Inc, 41 Hindmarsh Square, Adelaide, SA 5000. Tel: 08-223 4555

Royal Automobile Club of Tasmania, Corner Patrick & Murray Streets, Hobart, Tasmania 7000. Tel: 002-38 2200

Royal Automobile Club of Victoria (RACV) Ltd, 123 Queen Street, Melbourne, Victoria 3000. Tel: 03-607 2211

Royal Automobile Club of WA Inc, 228 Adelaide Terrace, Perth, WA 6000. Tel: 09-421 4444

Vehicle registration

The Registrar of Motor Vehicles, Department of Territories, PO Box 582, Dickson, ACT 2602.

The Registrar of Motor Vehicles, Department of Motor Transport, GPO Box 28, Sydney, NSW 2001.

The Motor Vehicle Registry, Department of Transport & Works, PO Box 530, Darwin, NT 5794.

The Manager, Motor Vehicle Registration Branch, Main Road Department, GPO Box 2451, Brisbane, Queensland 4001.

The Registrar of Motor Vehicles, Motor Registration Division, 60 Wakefield Street, Adelaide, SA 5000.

The Registrar of Motor Vehicles, GPO Box 1002K, Hobart, Tasmania 7001.

The Road Traffic Authority, Vehicle Engineering, PO Box 119, Carlton South, Victoria 3053.

The Manager, Police Department, Licensing & Services Section, 22 Mount Street, Perth, WA 6000.

Other organisations

Australian Institute of Multicultural Affairs, GPO Box 2470V, Melbourne, Victoria 3001. Tel: 01-608 1777

Australian Overseas Student Office, Department of Education, PO Box 25, Woden, ACT 2606.

Department of Immigration & Ethnic Affairs, Central Office, Benjamin Offices, Chan Street, Belconnen, ACT 2617. Tel: 062-64 1111

Department of Social Security, Juliana House, Bowes Street, Phillip, ACT 2606. Tel: 062-89 1444

Department of Trade, Edmund Barton Building, Kings Avenue, Barton, ACT 2600. Tel: 062-72 3911

Federation of Ethnic Communities' Councils of Australia, 5th Floor, 541 George Street, Sydney, NSW 2000. Tel: 02-2679722

Immigration Advice & Rights Centre, 48-50 Darcy Street, Parramatta, NSW 2150. Tel: 01-608 6871

International Education Branch, Dept of Education, PO Box 826, Woden, ACT 2606

United Kingdom Settlers Association, PO Box 221, Fitzroy, Victoria 3065. Tel: 03-4193788

Index

190